D1715611

THE FINEST BUILDING IN AMERICA

THE FINEST
BUILDING IN
AMERICA

THE NEW YORK CRYSTAL PALACE
1853–1858

EDWIN G. BURROWS

OXFORD
UNIVERSITY PRESS

OXFORD
UNIVERSITY PRESS

Oxford University Press is a department of the University of Oxford.
It furthers the University's objective of excellence in research, scholarship,
and education by publishing worldwide. Oxford is a registered trade mark of
Oxford University Press in the UK and certain other countries.

Published in the United States of America by Oxford University Press
198 Madison Avenue, New York, NY 10016, United States of America.

Library of Congress Cataloging in Publication Data
Names: Burrows, Edwin G., 1943– author.
Title: The finest building in America : the New York Crystal Palace,
1853–1858 / Edwin G. Burrows.
Description: New York : Oxford University Press, 2018.
Identifiers: LCCN 2017031341 | ISBN 9780190681210 (hardback)
Subjects: LCSH: Crystal Palace (New York, N.Y.) | New York Exhibition
of the Industry of All Nations (1853–1854 : New York, N.Y.) | Glass
construction—New York (State)—New York. | Lost architecture—New York
(State)—New York. | New York (N.Y.)—Buildings, structures, etc. | New
York (N.Y.)—History—1775–1865. | BISAC: HISTORY / General. | HISTORY /
United States / State & Local / Middle Atlantic (DC, DE, MD, NJ, NY, PA).
Classification: LCC NA6750.N5 B87 2018 | DDC 721/.0449609747—dc23 LC
record available at https://lccn.loc.gov/2017031341

1 3 5 7 9 8 6 4 2
Printed by CTPS, China

For Pat, Matt, & Kate

You have also seen our own New-York grow
from a provincial town to a vast metropolis, heaving in its heart
with the pulsations of a world, and wearing its
Crystal Palace like a diadem.

NEW-YORK DAILY TRIBUNE, MAY 5, 1854

CONTENTS

The End

Around five o'clock in the afternoon of October 5, 1858, thick black smoke boiled out of a storeroom in the Crystal Palace on New York's Reservoir Square (now Bryant Park), an exhibition venue renowned throughout the United States for its pioneering use of iron and glass as well as for hosting the first American World's Fair. Moments later, witnesses saw a "sudden flash," after which flames began to flow like lava across the varnished pine floors of the interior galleries, curling up toward the building's central dome and "whirling round in terrible eddies." Panicked by cries of "Fire! Fire!" the several thousand visitors inside rushed for the exits, "crying and screaming in the most pitiable manner" while a giant steam calliope, oblivious to the pandemonium, pumped out "Pop

Goes the Weasel." Women fainted and tumbled down flights of stairs. Parents lost track of their children. The aged and infirm were bowled over in the stampede. A quick-thinking engineer attempted to extinguish the flames by releasing the steam from some nearby boilers, while a few stalwart men grabbed the fire hoses attached to hydrants at strategic locations on the ground floor. But the steam proved insufficient, or the hoses were full of holes, or the water pressure was too low (explanations varied), and they were all soon driven back by heat so intense that cast-iron girders began snapping "like brittle glass." Others reportedly took advantage of the confusion to make off with jewelry, watches, silverware, and other objects of value on display.[1]

Barely fifteen minutes after the initial alarm had been raised, flames enveloped the dome, throwing "great waves of lurid light" over a throng of spectators who had quickly filled the streets outside. Policemen from nearby precincts struggled to control the crowd, seizing a number of pickpockets in the bargain. The dome then collapsed with a "tremendous crash," taking down the remainder of the roof and causing the outer walls to cave in. Inside half an hour the Crystal Palace had been reduced to a heap of smoldering debris. It was later found that a whirlwind created by the heat of the fire had swept pieces of the tin roof across the East River to Long Island, three miles away. George Templeton Strong, the diarist, raced to the scene and watched "a majestic column of smoke" rise into the blue sky, "wreathing and flowing" downtown on the early evening breeze. As the sun set, the smoke floated over St. John's Park, puzzling residents like the young Morgan Dix, the future rector of Trinity Church, who did not learn until the next day where it came from.[2]

Firemen allegedly pulled a corpse from the ruins that same evening, giving rise to somewhat hysterical predictions—fed by rumors of people who had gone missing in the melee—that more bodies would turn up. But none ever did. Subsequent investigation determined that there had been no corpse after all, and that by some miracle everyone had escaped the building without serious injury. Hundreds of workingmen, inventors, artists, and manufacturers exhibiting their work at the annual show of the American Institute were completely ruined nonetheless. Estimates of the loss in property exceeded one million dollars, equal in 2015 to as little as $22 million and as much as $4.4 *billion*.[3]

"The conflagration of the Crystal Palace was the great city fact," observed the *Times* a couple of days later—"nothing else was thought of"—and much speculation ensued about how any fire could have started in an iron building widely believed to be fireproof. Many people thought that the fire's surprising speed and intensity pointed to arson, although there was no agreement as to the identity of the culprit or culprits. One eyewitness

xii   *The Finest Building in America*

remembered seeing "two or three boys" running pell-mell down 42nd Street after the first alarm had been raised. Another saw a man in a dark coat exiting the storeroom about the same time with his hat pulled suspiciously down so as to conceal his face. Still others spoke of smelling gas, camphene, or turpentine in the same area, evidence "that there must have been villanous [sic] work in the matter." As for a possible motive, the *Tribune* pointed out that property owners in the neighborhood had wanted the Crystal Palace removed because of the "grog-shops and other disreputable establishments" it attracted. "Suffice it to say," the paper concluded darkly, "their end is attained." Hefty rewards were offered for the arrest and conviction of the "remorseless wretch" responsible for the blaze.

Not everyone assumed an arsonist was to blame. Another eyewitness told the *Tribune* that he heard someone say, "they are going to light the gas," after which he heard the cry of "fire, fire." Almost immediately thereafter,

I saw streams of fire like snakes running in all directions through the building and setting it on fire nearly as fast as a man could run. The color of the smoke, the intensity of flame, and two or three small explosions, forces the idea to my mind that, to save a few dollars, the gas pipes of the Crystal Palace had only been gutta percha [latex] instead of wrought iron tubes; and that shortly after the gas was turned on there was a

leak somewhere in [the] rear of the north nave which set fire
to the gas tubes . . . [which] was the true and legitimate cause
of this lamentable disaster.

The next day, when he returned to the ruins and searched for
signs of iron tubing, this witness said he could find nary a one.
Until he had reason to think otherwise, he preferred his theory
that the fire began with a ruptured gutta-percha gas line. A
representative of the firm that installed them swore under oath,
however, that all 30,000 feet of the lines were made of wrought
iron with lead fittings and regularly inspected. After sifting
through this and other contradictory testimony, the *Times*
agreed that an incendiary must have been responsible for the
fire as there was no credible evidence of "any oversight, care-
lessness or accident of those within the building." Even so,
subsequent investigation by the authorities failed to produce a
suspect or suspects, much less a motive, and to this day the cause
of the conflagration remains unclear.

·······

What is clear is that the fire made a profound impression on
everyone who saw it. A visitor from out West declared that
he had watched "steamboats in flames" as well as "prairies on
fire," but nothing remotely like the burning of the Crystal

Palace in New York. "Grand and sublime," exclaimed a city resident—*sublime* being a word favored in those days for great scenes that could not be called *beautiful* but nonetheless inspired awe, incredulity, and even trepidation. Others spoke of the scene's "awful grandeur"—of "a splendid and exciting spectacle"—"magnificent and sublime beyond anything that I ever witnessed"—"grand and sublime, presenting the most magnificent spectacle ever witnessed in this city"—"truly grand and at the same time terrific," declared a Brooklyn man, himself probably one of the exhibitors wiped out by the fire, who watched the whole thing on the ferry home.[4]

"All who witnessed the spectacle," wrote a reporter for the *Herald*, "declare that it was one of those things rarely seen in a lifetime." The *Times* called it "one of the most disastrous conflagrations that New-York has been visited with in a long time," adding, "The calamity has struck everyone aghast, for the possibility of such an event has never been calculated upon. The peculiar character of the building, constructed as it was almost entirely of iron and glass, appeared to bid defiance to the flames, yet its destruction was more rapid than any building of wood could possibly have been." Even the *sound* of the inferno— "the cracking of glass, and roaring of wind & flames, as they rushed up through the roof and sides of the building"—was strange and unforgettable.

"The Crystal Palace is no more!" exclaimed the *American Phrenological Journal*. In minutes, that "immense and beautiful structure" had been utterly destroyed. Some doubted the city could ever recover. "We shall never have another Crystal Palace," fretted the *Tribune*. "Its glorious dome . . . is no more; its galleries, its treasures, its magnificent expanses indispensable to the mass-gatherings of this great metropolis—its superb memories are all gone, and gone forever." And not only New York will grieve: the destruction of the Crystal Palace would come as a "painful surprise" to people around the country—a "cause not only for local but national regret."

Within days of the fire, crews began cleaning up, carting off tons of rubbish. They finished quickly. Rainy weather discouraged looters, the crowds of onlookers dwindled, and soon the country was preoccupied with civil war. In time, it had bigger expositions elsewhere to gawk at as well. Even before Reservoir Square became Bryant Park, a leafy oasis in the concrete desert of midtown Manhattan, what had once been the most famous destination in the United States was all but forgotten. Historians haven't been much help, either, in preserving public memory of the Crystal Palace. It has been the subject of no more than a handful of scholarly articles and earns at best passing mention in a few standard narratives of the period.

.·◦◦●◦◦·.

This little book is my attempt to recapture the lost story of the New York Crystal Palace and to understand why this building mattered so much to antebellum Americans in general and New Yorkers in particular, yet would never be rebuilt. The explanation is partly one of colliding ambitions, miscalculations, incompetence, and mismanagement that no one wanted to go through a second time—in its account of the fire, *Scientific American* alluded cryptically to "a series of troubles and vicissitudes of no ordinary character." Others might prefer to call it the quintessential New York tale. It is also part of the larger narrative of how, seventy-five years after Independence, Americans cast off Revolutionary republicanism, which idealized a life of frugality and self-sufficient simplicity, and embraced the brave new world of industry, luxury, and the siren song of the marketplace.

While identifying and combining the various elements of this story, I had the undeserved good fortune to receive assistance, advice, and encouragement from patient friends, notably Peggy Brown, Ralph Brown, Don Gerardi, Paul Goodspeed, Michael Hattem, Matt Knutson, Bob Mutch, David Troyansky, Lindsay Turley, and Sharon Zukin. I trust they won't be too disappointed in the results. Special thanks as well to my agent, Sam Stoloff; to Tim Bent and Amy Whitmer at Oxford University Press; and to my collaborator of many years, Mike Wallace.

I have dedicated this book to my wife and children, architects of my own Crystal Palace.

ONE

Glances at Europe

AT THE END OF April 1851, the speedy new side-wheeler *Baltic*, twelve days out of New York, churned into Liverpool after a rough Atlantic crossing (Figure 1.1). Among her 204 bilious passengers was Horace Greeley, moon-faced editor of the *New-York Daily Tribune* and celebrated friend of labor, promoter of industrialism and invention, champion of reform (temperance, women's rights, abolition), and advocate of cooperative socialism (Figure 1.2). Though grateful to have survived "the perils and miseries of the raging main," as he put it, the American newspaperman promptly caught a train to London—not necessarily a safer mode of transportation, given that exploding boilers and catastrophic derailments were still common in those early days of rail travel. But Greeley was in

[FIGURE 1.1] The USS *Baltic*, one of four transatlantic steamships belonging to the new Collins line. Months after Greeley's trip to the Great Exhibition, she made the Atlantic crossing in under ten days—a record that stood for years. Edward Collins, founder of the line, later served on the board of the Crystal Palace Association in New York. (Courtesy of the Library of Congress)

a hurry. He needed to be in London on the first of May, only a day or two away, when Queen Victoria and Prince Albert would open the Great Exhibition of the Works of Industry of All Nations, the first world's fair, in Hyde Park.[1]

Exhibitions as such were nothing new. In England, they had been used to promote domestic manufacturing since the middle of the previous century, and there was a group in Paris called the Temple of Industry that put one on every few years or so. But this was to be an event of unprecedented scope and magnitude. Henry Cole, one of its organizers, promised to put on "a festival such as the world has never seen."[2]

Not surprisingly, given the breadth of this vision, the Great Exhibition would mean different things to different people. Some thought its emphasis on innovation and good design would raise standards of production while improving public "taste," which in practice often meant stoking consumer demand for manufactured goods. Others thought the sheer quantity of objects (ultimately more than half of which came from Britain itself) would provide tangible evidence that British manufacturing already outstripped that of other nations and defined what it meant to be "modern." Still others expected the Exhibition to underscore the power and reach of the new British Empire by summoning goods from distant provinces, along with luxuries from workshops throughout the so-called civilized world, then assembling them under one roof. Prince Albert himself hoped the Exhibition would advance the cause of international peace by promoting free trade and friendly competition among nations instead of protectionism and its inevitable outcome, war. It's not always clear what ordinary visitors thought, although almost everyone seems to have had a good time.[3]

Arguably the most prominent American to attend the Great Exhibition, Greeley was also one of the most vocal proponents

of the idea, now almost axiomatic among many of his compa-
triots, that it was an opportunity to show not simply the abun-
dant natural resources or agricultural prowess of the country,
but how industrialization would improve the lives of working
people. By the time he boarded the *Baltic*, upbeat progress reports in the *Tribune* as well as other papers had already helped
to make the fair an urgent topic in the United States—
"watched and discussed," Greeley would assert, "not more earnestly throughout the saloons of Europe, than by the smith's
forge and the mechanic's bench in America."[4]

◦∘◦▒◦∘◦

Adding to the hoopla were eye-popping accounts of the building erected to house the Exhibition. Designed by Joseph
Paxton, a farmer's son, currently the Duke of Devonshire's
head gardener, and a man with a gift for innovative architecture,

LEFT [FIGURE 1.2] Horace Greeley, portrait by Matthew Brady, ca. 1844–1860.
In early 1852, when Greeley was on the road lecturing on "The Crystal Palace and
Its Lessons"—later collected into a book of the same title—a friendly editor
described the "threadbare white coat," broken-down hat, scuffed boots,
"intellectual head," and "milk-white face" for which Greeley had become famous.
When they met a couple of years later, Lord Acton thought Greeley "a very
strange-looking man, half cracked and half a rogue." (*The Barre Patriot,* Jan. 23,
1852; "Lord Acton's American Diaries," *Fortnightly Review*, 110 (1921), 739.)
(Image courtesy of the Library of Congress)

[FIGURE 1.3] The Crystal Palace, Hyde Park, London. Depictions of its New York counterpart would often place it in a similarly bucolic setting, surrounded by grass and trees. (*Dickinson's Comprehensive Pictures of the Great Exhibition of 1851.* Courtesy of the Smithsonian Libraries.)

it resembled nothing so much as an enormous greenhouse or railway shed, better than 600 yards long and 150 wide, made up of a million plate glass panels set in prefabricated iron frames and bolted together. When completed in a mere seven months, it covered almost nineteen acres and would contain 13,000 exhibits from forty nations around the world (Figure 1.3). It was also high enough (at 108 feet) to enclose spectacular fountains and several full-grown elms. People dubbed it the Crystal Palace, and by all accounts it was as worth seeing as anything in the Exhibition. Greeley himself trumpeted the Crystal Palace as the perfect symbol of modern, industrial society—a new kind of building for a new kind of world. It was, he would write, "one of the noblest, most magnificent, most graceful edifices ever seen" and the beginning of a revolution in architecture. "Depend on it," he prophesied, "stone and timber will have to stand back for iron and glass hereafter, to an extent not yet conceivable." Almost everybody who saw it had the same reaction (Figure 1.4).[5]

The Crystal Palace had to be "the most marvellous edifice in the world," gushed the *Brooklyn Eagle*. Under its former editor, Walt Whitman, the paper had wanted exhibitions to instruct and improve the masses. Now it could scarcely contain its enthusiasm for Paxton's building in London, declaring that "There has been nothing to compare with it for grace, lightness, fancy, and variety of effects as the sun is crossed by moving clouds." Similarly, an enraptured visitor from Philadelphia wrote of the building's "great arch, which sprang like a silver bow aloft, while the symmetrical naves swept

FOLLOWING PAGE [FIGURE 1.4] Interior view of the north transept, Crystal Palace. The first of a series of color lithographs prepared for Prince Albert, this view of the north transept shows the huge glass fountain, silhouetted against one of the two elms, at the center of the exhibition. Note the sculpture at the base of each column and the galleries above. "The view from near the end close to the last entrance," Queen Victoria wrote in her diary, "one can never, never carry in one's mind—each time one is amazed afresh at the immense length and height and the fairy-like effect of the different objects that fill it" (quoted in Gibbs-Smith, *Great Exhibition*, 20). (*Dickinson's Comprehensive Pictures of the Great Exhibition of 1851.* Courtesy of the Smithsonian Libraries.)

softly away in the distance, and left its impress indelibly upon the soul." Quoting first Milton and then the Bible, Yale's Benjamin Silliman observed how " 'It rose like an exhalation,' a magical illusion of the senses. The framework of iron, although strong enough to sustain weight and to resist the winds, is so little apparent to the eye, that the Crystal Palace appears a sea of glass, as in Revelations, 'A sea of glass like unto crystal.' " The Reverend Cleveland Coxe of Baltimore, who initially dismissed the Crystal Palace as "a mere toy of Prince Albert's," changed his tune when he saw it for himself:

> The crystal roof showered a soft daylight over the immense interior; the trees and curious plants gave it a cheerful and varied beauty; the eye bewildered itself in a maze of striking objects of luxury and taste; musical instruments, constantly playing, bewitched the ear, their tones blending from various distances and directions, in a kind of harmonious discord; fountains were gurgling and scattering their spray, like diamonds and pearls, and the rank and pride of England mixed with the auxiliary representatives of foreign states....

As the excitement mounted on both sides of the Atlantic, hotels, railroads, and steamship companies reportedly planned special excursion packages for curious tourists. London shopkeepers tried to lure visitors from the States by advertising their wares in American newspapers. A children's book called *The Crystal Palace: A Little Book for Little Boys* was in press by 1851, while later that same year P. T. Barnum would draw appreciative crowds in New York with his "GRAND MOVING PICTURE OF THE CRYSTAL PALACE"—a slowly revolving panorama that he called a "progressive mirror"—at Stoppani Hall on Broadway. Wall Street brokers planned a ticket raffle, and con artists reportedly bilked out-of-towners with promises to take them to London and back for a mere $100. A story went around that "one hundred young gentlemen of New York have purchased or chartered a ship to come to the great exhibition." They will anchor in the Thames, "live on board, give parties, &c., &c." Even Vice President Millard Fillmore said he wanted to see the Exhibition for himself, but shelved his plans after the sudden death of President Zachary Taylor in July 1850.[6]

Ultimately, of the 6½ million people who attended the Exhibition before it closed in mid-October, almost 6,000 were purportedly sightseeing Americans—a tiny fraction of the total, though far more than would have been possible before the advent of steamships and railroads. "[N]ow such are the advantages for rapid travelling by steam," asserted a reflective Vermont editor, "that a person in the interior of this country can go to its shores, and then cross the vast ocean of several thousands of miles in extent, and appear at the place of that great exhibition in the short space of two or three weeks; and on this rapidity of travelling is founded the fair prospect of so magnificent a scheme as the world's exhibition." He might have mentioned that the demand for accommodations and food had driven London prices to unprecedented highs, too. A correspondent of the *Tribune* calculated that a comfortable excursion from the States, "without looking so very sharp after the pennies," could now cost up to $500 per person—the equivalent in purchasing power of at least $16,000 in 2015.[7]

Not that the Great Exhibition lacked for critics, especially in England itself. There were complaints about Paxton's unorthodox design for the building, complaints about locating it in a park favored by the fashionable classes, complaints about the great expense that would inevitably be required to construct it, complaints that it would fall down in the first wind, complaints about the space allocated to this or that nation, complaints that too many of the exhibits consisted of useless curiosities. Opponents alleged that Free Trade would open the door to bearded foreigners burdened (like the French) with more primitive ideas about hygiene than the English, exposing Londoners to all kinds of diseases. What was more, inviting great crowds into the capital would provoke violent disturbances reminiscent of the Chartist upheavals during the 1840s—in the Reverend Coxe's words, that "something revolutionary and bloody might be the result of the collection of vast bodies of men, with a large proportion of foreign republicans among them, into the bosom of the Metropolis."[8]

Talk like that exasperated Prince Albert, who confided to his grandmother that some people appear to believe the Exhibition will attract foreigners seeking only "to commence a thorough revolution here, to murder Victoria and myself and to proclaim the Red Republic in England."[9]

These fears of a proletarian uprising were not entirely far-fetched. As recently as 1848 the propertied classes had watched in horror as rioting broke out in city after city across the Continent. In France, long feared as the epicenter of radicalism, crowds brought down another French king and established the Second Republic; soon they would rally to the Second Empire of Louis Napoléon, evidence in certain precincts that the masses were dangerously fickle and irrational. Meanwhile, in London, worried men stacked sandbags around the Bank of England and put guns on its roof, while the government took the precaution of moving several regiments of soldiers into the capital. Less than three years later, with riot and revolution still hanging in the air like smoke, the prospect of hundreds of thousands—millions—of people crowding into the city to see an industrial exhibition looked like perfect madness. Some of her advisers thought the queen should leave town for the duration. The aging Duke of Wellington urged the government to station a contingent of cavalry in Hyde Park. Respectable people were not comforted to learn that numbers of revolutionary socialists from Austria and Prussia had fled to London in recent years, most notably Karl Marx, co-author of *The Communist Manifesto* (1848), who now spent his days studying history and economics in the British Library. No matter that he wanted nothing to do with the Exhibition, which he dismissed as a perfect illustration of capitalist commodity fetishism.[10]

~••◦◦••~

Greeley reached London in time to join the flood of people—30,000 season ticket holders inside the Crystal Palace along with perhaps ten times that number outside—who witnessed the royal procession launching the Exhibition. In letters intended for readers of the *Tribune*, published the following year as *Glances at Europe*, he marveled at the good behavior of the opening crowd, so different from the raucous free-for-all that one could expect from a big public gathering back in the States—and conspicuously unlike the hostile, crazed mob that some had predicted.

The pomp and ceremony were something else altogether. The locals mostly loved it, of course. According to one typically breathless account: "Unquestionably neither Eastern fairy tale nor Arabian Nights wonder could surpass, or even emulate the gorgeous reality that greets the delighted gaze of the assembled spectators, as the royal party and brilliant cortege advanced through the bronzed and gilded gates that led into this hall of enchantment."[11]

Horace Greeley, the republican from America, was unimpressed. "Our New York Fire Department could beat it," he yawned; "so could our Odd-Fellows."[12]

Indeed, Greeley found something disturbingly incongruous about the entire spectacle. What did a hereditary monarch, attended by grooms and ushers and ladies-in-waiting and other such "uncouth fossils" of a bygone era, have to do with the achievements of modern industry? "In the age of the Locomotive and the Telegraph," he wrote, "royalty itself is an anachronism." All those pampered aristocrats in Victoria's entourage were merely "the descendants of some Norman robbers, none of whom ever contemplated the personal doing of any real work as even a remote possibility, and any of whom would feel insulted by a report that his father or grandfather invented the Steam Engine or Spinning Jenny." And where, he wondered, were the inventors, architects, engineers, craftsmen, and common laborers who did all the work? They, not the doddering remnants of an obsolete social order, should be in the line of march, savoring the cheers of grateful multitudes.[13]

Over the next several weeks, Greeley prowled the aisles of the Crystal Palace nearly every day. He ogled steam-powered machinery, inspected minerals and clocks and kitchen appliances and tapestries, hobnobbed with dignitaries, and chaired a panel of judges for the Hardware Department. He grew ever-more certain that the Great Exhibition—"this marvellous achievement of Human Genius, Skill, Taste, and Industry"—this "magnificent temple of Art"—this "great Test Ground of the World's ingenuity, skill and knowledge"—would only hasten the day when labor finally received its fair measure of dignity and happiness. But how could a collection of mere objects bring about so fundamental a change in culture and social re-lations? "Skilled artisans or sharp-eyed apprentices," Greeley reasoned, would leave the Exhibition inspired by new ideas; then, applying these ideas to the continuing improvement of production, they would "speedily transform the Industrial and Social condition of mankind." Shoes, for example, could be made faster and more cheaply by machine. Clothing, too: Why sew seams by hand "when machinery can do the work even better and twenty times as fast"? In fact, Greeley contin-ued, "I shall be disappointed if this Exhibition be not speedily followed by immense advances in Labor-Saving Machinery."

He had seen the future, and it worked.[14]

-·●●●●·-

For its part, the American contribution to the Crystal Palace exhibition got off to a disappointing start. "No nation could

have sent thither as varied, interesting, and important specimens of art and skill, and science and industry as the United
States," groused the *New-York Herald*. "But the federal government, or rather Congress, declined in making an appropri-
ation to aid in the transmission of the articles to the fair, or to
have anything to do with the matter." Instead, the secretary of
state invited the private National Institute for the Promotion
of Science and the Arts to form a Central Committee that
would in turn invite the state governors to appoint commissioners who would solicit and screen exhibitors.

The Central Committee cast its net widely, embracing a
definition of industrial production that would have struck
many people, Greeley among them, as unfortunate. "The productions of American industry which will be entitled to places
in the exhibition are not limited to articles of manufacturing,
mechanical or any other department of skill," the committee
declared in the autumn of 1850. "The farm, the garden and the
dairy, the forest and the mine, the factory and the workshop,
the laboratory and studio will all be entitled to their respec-
tive positions, and it is earnestly hoped that no consideration
will be allowed to prevent a full and honorable representation
of every department of our natural resources." The *Tribune*
dismissed the whole business as humbug.

Over the winter of 1850–51, this vague and decentralized
approach by the United States—probably unique among

participating nations—yielded comparatively few exhibits, chiefly the natural products that Greeley found so unimpressive. Early visitors to the American section of the Crystal Palace encountered hams, barrels of turpentine, steam-dried Indian corn, lard oil, Gothic windows made of transparent soap, Lauderback's preserved peaches, Borden's meat biscuits, Oswego pure starch, moss from New Orleans, and, from Vermont, a leaf. Regrettably, Greeley reported, "Our Manufacturers are in many departments grossly deficient"—reinforcing the common misconception that Americans are country bumpkins who don't, or can't, appreciate "the nicer processes of Art," i.e., how to make the useful things that would improve the lives of ordinary people. Worse, these dubious items took up only about half the space provided for all exhibits from the United States. *Punch* hooted in derision. "An enormous banner betokened the whole of the east end as devoted to the United States," said the famous satirical magazine (Figure 1.5). "But what was our astonishment, on arriving there, to find their contribution to the world's industry consists as yet of a few wine glasses, a square or two of soap, and a pair of salt-cellars! For a calculating people, our friends the Americans are thus far terribly out in their calculations."[15]

The sting of this "mortifying failure," as Greeley later put it, began to wear off as more American exhibitors arrived in London during the summer and fall of 1851 and British opinion shifted. There was a thrilling demonstration of Cyrus McCormick's mechanical reaper. Charles Goodyear displayed a range of products made with something he called vulcanized rubber. Samuel Colt showed off his six-shooter, and there were several examples of Samuel Morse's new telegraph. A representative of the American lock makers Day and Newell humiliated his British counterparts by picking their best lock, then selling his company's model to the Bank of England. From faraway Milwaukee came a machine that could dress up to 8,000 barrel staves a day. Now, visitors to the American section could also see a sewing machine, an ice-making machine, a candle-making machine, and a brick-making machine, along with machines for dressing hemp, rolling tin, printing books, cutting stone, and more.

As the Exhibition drew to a close in mid-October, the laughing had given way to grudging admiration. "Great Britain has received more useful ideas and more ingenious inventions from the United States, through the exhibition, than from all

FOLLOWING PAGE [FIGURE 1.5] The United States exhibit at the London Crystal Palace. "We could not help," said *Punch*, "being struck by the glaring contrast between large pretension and little performance, as exemplified in the dreary and *empty* aspect of the large space claimed by and allowed to America." Disappointment that the country had not put its best foot forward helped convince many Americans to mount another fair in New York. (*Dickinson's Comprehensive Pictures of the Great Exhibition of 1851*. Courtesy of the Smithsonian Libraries.)

other sources," conceded the *Times* of London. Said the *Liverpool Times*: "The Yankees are no longer to be ridiculed, much less despised."[16]

⋯⦿⦿⦿⋯

Greeley returned home on the *Baltic* in early August, satisfied that his countrymen were holding their own at the Great Exhibition, yet keenly aware as well that their showing "fell far short of what it might have been, and did not fairly exhibit the progress and present condition of the Useful Arts" in the United States. "Our real error consists, not in neglecting to send articles to rival the rich fabrics and wares of this Continent, but in sending too few of those homely but most important products in which we ɪunquestionably lead the world.... [W]e should have had many more." Next time, he vowed, "We can and must do better."[17]

It was already fairly certain, in fact, that there would *be* a next time. As early as February 1851—two months before Greeley left for Liverpool—there had been talk that a second exhibition would take place in New York in 1852, perhaps on Governors Island, just off lower Manhattan. A London correspondent for the *Boston Post* advised caution—events of importance shouldn't be thrown together too quickly, he said—but the Cleveland *Plain Dealer* noted that it too had heard of "a proposed World's Fair in 1852, to be held on Governors Island" and, like most people, thought it would be a very constructive experience for the country.

By January or February 1852, newspapers all over America were running notices of a fair planned for New York City in the near future. Greeley himself had already begun thinking along the same or similar lines. "I know well so large and diversified a show of Machinery could not be made up in the United States as is here presented in behalf of British Invention," he wrote after only a week in London. "Yet I think a strictly American Fair might be got up which would evince more originality of creation or design." Months later, while preparing his essays in the *Tribune* for publication, he remained committed to the idea. "I do hope we may have a Crystal Palace of like proportions in New York within two years," he interjected at one point. "It would be of inestimable worth as a study to our young architects, builders and artisans."[18]

Serious planning for a second fair in New York seems to have originated with the American Commissioner to the London exhibition, Edward Riddle. Appointed by the Whig Secretary of State Daniel Webster, Riddle was a somewhat obscure Boston carriage maker who believed fervently that manufacturing would fulfill the promise of democracy, and that the Crystal Palace exhibition in particular had demonstrated the superiority of American values and institutions. While

still in England, Riddle became friendly with a number of influential businessmen from the States who had exhibited at
the Crystal Palace. They wanted to do something similar but
permanent in America—because it had become a matter of
national pride, because the Hyde Park exhibition made a lot of
money, and because once it had closed as planned, the building
would be dismantled, leaving many exhibitors like themselves
to dispose of unsold merchandise. Importantly, everyone understood from the outset that an undertaking of this nature
could only take place in New York City.[19]

•••••

By 1850, having cooled off for a decade after the Panic of 1837,
New York's economy had warmed up again and the city was well
on its way to becoming the dominant metropolitan center in the
country. With a population on the far side of 650,000 and
rising fast—in 1860 the number of its inhabitants would
exceed 1,000,000—New York was already bigger and growing faster than any rival. It had long since become the nation's
most active port of entry for immigrants, receiving upwards of
several hundred thousand newcomers, three of every four,
each year. Its merchant-princes steered ever-larger shares of
southern cotton and Midwestern grain onto world markets,
ultimately cornering a third of the nation's exports a well as

half its imports. New York bankers and brokers drew record numbers of investors at home and abroad into the city's capital markets to finance ramifying networks of railroad, steamship, and telegraph lines, ensuring that "Wall Street" would be as well known, and reviled, on the Mississippi as on the Hudson. Newspapers and magazines from New York were read in the rough-and-tumble mining camps of California as well as in the genteel townhouses clustered around Manhattan's lower Fifth Avenue, Union Square, Waverly Place, and Washington Square—swank residential quarters where an affluent urban bourgeoisie lived in greater comfort and convenience than previous generations of Americans could have imagined. According to one estimate, mid-century New York could boast of ten men worth at least $500,000 each—equivalent to some $16 million in 2014 dollars; twenty-five years earlier there had been two.

While the rich kept getting richer, the poor got poorer—and every year there were a lot more of them. In 1845, just as the great boom was getting under way, Greeley himself estimated that as many as two-thirds of the city's inhabitants were impoverished and 50,000 people lived on the brink of starvation; a couple of years later, the author of *Life in New York* raised that number to 75,000. At a time when some big men in town already reckoned their wealth in millions, a shoemaker earned less than $5.00 per week; a seamstress might earn $1.25. Nearly half the population was foreign-born, and not surprisingly, a sizable majority of the poor consisted of Irish and German immigrants who found shelter in the squalid Five Points section or one of the grim shantytowns north of the city. But they were everywhere. The poor, the *Tribune* had said in 1847, inhabited "every hole and corner under a roof, down to [New York's] very vaults and cellars."[20]

‹‹‹●●●●●››

In December 1851, now back in the States, Riddle began recruiting New Yorkers with deep pockets and an interest in an American Crystal Palace. Among them were individuals with ties to one firm in particular, the Liverpool and London Fire and Life Insurance Company, among them August Belmont, Alexander Hamilton Jr., Alfred Pell, and Mortimer Livingston. Organized as the Association for the Exhibition of the Industry of All Nations, Riddle and friends petitioned the New York City Common Council for permission to build in Madison Square, a six-acre plot on 23rd Street that had been officially designated as a park only a few years earlier and was already known for its lovely elms, oaks, and sycamores. The Council readily agreed. But respectable people who lived near the new park feared they would be overrun by riffraff. They sued to have the Council's decision overturned. The

Court of Appeals ruled in their favor, whereupon the aldermen gave Riddle a five-year lease on Reservoir Square, a desolate one-time potter's field facing Sixth Avenue between 40th and 42nd Streets and next to the hulking Croton Distributing Reservoir—"a desert of rocks and untamed lots," scoffed the *Times*, "with goats feeding at random"—larger than Madison Square by several acres but so far uptown that no one could possibly object (or so they thought). Besides, almost everyone calculated that a world's fair would promote speedy development of the neighborhood (Figure 1.6). The Council's only two requirements were that the Association's building be constructed of iron and glass like the Crystal Palace in London and that the entrance fee should not exceed fifty cents.[21]

(The Council had area residents up in arms again in the spring of 1853, only months before the Crystal Palace opened, by agreeing to let a showman named Henri Franconi build a 10,000-seat hippodrome on the west side of Fifth Avenue, directly across from Madison Square. For the next several years, during which time he reportedly liked to ride up and down Broadway on an ostrich, he treated New Yorkers to circus acts, gymnastic demonstrations, candlelight chariot races, historical re-enactments, musical performances, ballet, and other entertainments. Franconi's neighbors, on the other hand, complained that his shows attracted a distressing number of pickpockets, toughs, and con men. In 1856, the Hippodrome

went broke and was demolished to make way for the Fifth Avenue Hotel.)[22]

Maybe because he was irked at having been banished to the outskirts of town, or maybe because his pecuniary motives were criticized harshly in the press, Riddle sold out to a new group of investors reportedly for a generous $10,000—equivalent to at least $320,000 in 2015—and disappeared from the scene. ("This was cool and bright, was it not?" snickered *Scientific American*, dubbing him "the conspicuous, enterprising, know-how-to-make-money Edward Riddle.") By mid-March 1852, armed with a charter of incorporation from the state legislature, the board of directors had opened an office downtown at 53 Broadway. Officially, they were still the Association for the Exhibition of the Industry of All Nations, but everyone knew them by now as the Crystal Palace Association. The charter allowed the new corporation to issue stock up to $300,000.

LEFT [FIGURE 1.6 a and b] The Croton Reservoir, on the Dripps Map of 1851 (top), and the view south down Fifth Avenue (gouache by Augustus Fay, 1850). The Crystal Palace would be erected to the right, on the Reservoir's Sixth Avenue side, when Manhattan above 42nd Street was still a largely treeless wasteland of ungraded streets, truck farms, shanties, and empty lots. It did not even have street railway service along Sixth Avenue and Eighth Avenue until just before the Crystal Palace opened in 1853. Rich men were starting to build mansions and clubhouses along lower Fifth Avenue, but few had as yet ventured above 30th Street. The only other building of note in the area was the Colored Orphans Asylum on Fifth Avenue and 43rd Street, burned by a mob during the Draft Riots in 1863. (Courtesy of the New York Public Library)

Pell, Hamilton, and Livingston continued as directors of the reorganized Association. Joining them now were eight men who represented a somewhat broader cross section of the rich and accomplished: Johnston Livingston (a trustee of the American Express Company), John E. Devlin (a Boston merchant and apparently the sole non–New Yorker in the mix), Elbert J. Anderson (banker and sometime trustee of the New York and Erie Railroad), Francis W. Edmonds (the painter and cashier of the Mechanics Bank), Charles A. Stetson (manager of the famous Astor House and president of the esteemed Ohio Life Insurance and Trust Company), Philip Burrowes (a successful bankruptcy attorney), and Henry C. Murphy (the Brooklyn lawyer and historian). Theodore Sedgwick, a well-known New York attorney and brother of the writer Catharine Maria Sedgwick, was elected president (Figure 1.7). The new board seems to have met with public approval, inasmuch as

RIGHT [FIGURE 1.7] Theodore Sedgwick, president of the Crystal Palace Association. *Scientific American* called him "a most excellent man [who] does the best he possibly can, but he does not possess the tact and management indispensable for carrying out the erection of a building like this. What the Association most need, is a thoroughly practical and experienced managing head—such a man as Barnum, for instance—who can pull, push, coax, or drive, as occasion requires; and who is accustomed to the control and direction of numbers of workmen" (*Scientific American*, Apr. 9, 1853). Years later, he and the other directors of the Association would be remembered as "well-dressed, well-fed, jolly-countenanced men" (William G. Le Duc, "Minnesota at the Crystal Palace Exhibition," 364, Minnesota Historical Bulletin, vol.1). (Image courtesy of the Library of Congress)

Association stock sold out quickly and avid speculators on the Exchange soon drove the price up to $175 for a $100 share.[23]

Prior to Riddle's departure, the Association had come under fire for its cozy relations with private "auctioneers and stockjobbers," in the words of *Scientific American*, when the exhibition ought to be a public, national, and not-for-profit undertaking. Their "small and ridiculous copy of the Crystal Palace" in Hyde Park "will disgrace us in the eyes of the world," it went on. "We want no such exhibition in this city, nor in our country." Accusations like this dogged the Association for years, seasoned with generous amounts of anti–New York bitterness. In 1853, for example, the *Richmond Inquirer* would dismiss the Crystal Palace as a "contemptible humbug," contrived to let big city merchants, faro dealers, and pickpockets profit from a "stream of loose cash which the Crystal Palace is sucking in from every quarter of the country." Southerners in particular were victimized. "We have been caught," the paper admitted. "Thousands of inquisitive people from the South have traveled to New York through dust and heat; have suffered the torments of an over-crowded city; had their pockets picked, their persons searched, their toes mutilated, and for what?…In fine, the whole thing was miserably stale, flat and unprofitable. But it served its purpose. It put money in the pockets of Mr. Theodore Sedgewick [sic] & Co. It attracted an immense number of visitors from all parts of the country, and thus augmented the current cash of Gotham."[24]

In the summer of 1852, the Association sponsored a competition for the design of a glass and iron building to rival the original Crystal Palace. Judging the submissions was a committee of consulting engineers, which included John A. Roebling, manufacturer of wire rope, later renowned as the builder of the Brooklyn Bridge. The committee disqualified a plan sent in from London by Joseph Paxton himself because its elongated shape was wrong for Reservoir Square (Figure 1.8). Another, from the celebrated American landscape architect

[FIGURE 1.8] Joseph Paxton's plan for the Crystal Palace in New York envisioned a structure 600 feet long and 200 feet wide but similar in appearance and construction to its Hyde Park counterpart. A London paper observed, "The design is, on the whole, remarkable for its simplicity and practicability, and is another proof of Sir Joseph Paxton's great skill in this department of art" (quoted in the *Scientific American*, Jan. 17, 1851). (B. Silliman and C. R. Goodrich, eds., *The World of Science, Art, and Industry, Illustrated from Examples in the New-York Exhibition, 1853–54*. Courtesy of Columbia University Libraries.)

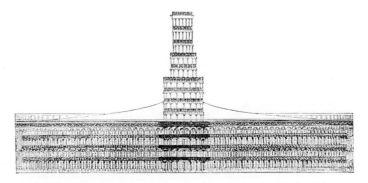

[FIGURE 1.9] The Bogardus design for the New York Crystal Palace. Its base consisted of a huge circular hall, 400 feet in diameter, ringed by a four-story self-supporting cast-iron exterior wall. At its center was a thirteen-story, 300-foot-high cast-iron circular tower, inside of which was a steam-powered elevator that would carry visitors up to an observatory at the top. Linked chains from the tower supported the sheet-iron roof of the hall. *Scientific American* campaigned hard for Bogardus, claiming that his design was "superior in all its details to the London Crystal Palace.... It is so planned that none of the braces and binders, which so disfigured the interior of Paxton's great work, will be required; it will be simple, yet beautiful and grand—a design original and unique, one worthy of our country...and it will never leak" (*Scientific American*, Feb. 12, 1852; see also *Scientific American*, Jul. 31, 1852). (*The World of Science, Art, and Industry, Illustrated from Examples in the New-York Exhibition, 1853–54*. Courtesy of Columbia University Libraries.)

Andrew Jackson Downing (submitted just prior to his death in a steamboat explosion), failed to pass muster because it used too much wood and canvas and not enough glass and iron, as stipulated by the city (Figure 1.9). James Bogardus, a New York contractor who had already started to build with iron, sent in a plan for a circular building with a suspension roof that resembled the Roman Coliseum (Figure 1.10).

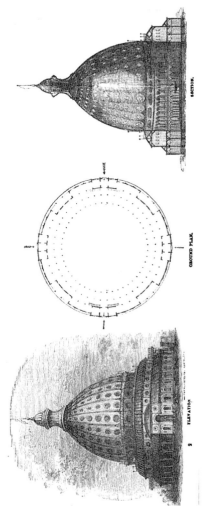

[FIGURE 1.10] Downing's vision of a Crystal Palace for New York—a design "of great novelty and bold conception," even though the dome was constructed of wood and canvas. (*The World of Science, Art, and Industry, Illustrated from Examples in the New-York Exhibition, 1853–54*. Courtesy of Columbia University Libraries.)

Scientific American greatly admired Bogardus's scheme, lauding him as a pioneer of cast-iron building, which he surely was, and making him out to be the only one of the lot who knew what he was doing. But after lengthy deliberation the committee judged his design too risky. In August 1852 they chose instead a proposal from two foreigners, Georg Carstensen and his partner, Karl Gildemeister (Figure 1.11). The 40-year-old Carstensen was a former officer in the Danish army, sometime songwriter (*Go-Ahead-American-Forward-Galop*), and one of the founders

[FIGURE 1.11a and b] Georg Carstensen and Charles Gildemeister. Perhaps best known today as one of the architects of the Tivoli Gardens in Copenhagen, Carstensen served as an officer in the Danish army before coming to New York around 1850. He returned to Copenhagen in 1855 and died two years later at the age of 44. He never knew that the Crystal Palace in New York had been destroyed by fire. Gildemeister, on the other hand, left New York in 1857 and may have known. (*New York Times*, Dec. 17, 1880.)

of the celebrated Tivoli Gardens in Copenhagen. Gildemeister was a 32-year-old trained architect who had fled his native Bremen, Germany, after the revolutions of 1848.

·························

With the plan the two architects had worked up, Carstensen submitted an explanation of why they disliked the site for the proposed exhibition building. "I could not," he wrote, "but be vividly impressed with the disadvantages of the locality, when compared with that of the Crystal Palace of London, which admitted of a free view of the edifice from all directions, besides being of unlimited extent, and affording natural auxiliaries in point of picturesqueness that are entirely wanting on Reservoir Square." (A defect that would be corrected in subsequent depictions of the Crystal Palace.) Besides the square's "prosy bareness" and the "restricted space" available for construction, the architects would have to contend with the massive, "fortress-like" Croton Reservoir looming in the background. Therefore, Carstensen reasoned, if the New York Crystal Palace were to be compared favorably with its London counterpart, it must rely on "the charms of novelty and originality, and thus escape the stigmatizing ridicule of being a miniature imitation of something much superior." Paxton had the advantage of building in an established, spacious park;

because he and Gildemeister had a more difficult assignment, they needed to come up with something truly special.[25]

With the shortcomings of Reservoir Square in mind, the two men proposed an octagonal iron and glass building "mostly on the Venetian style" but in the form of a Greek cross capped by a central dome (Figures 1.12 and 1.13). Supported by an ingenious system of columns, trusses, and tie rods, the dome's iron ribs would be covered with curved oak boards sheathed with tin. A lantern (cupola) on top allowed additional light into the interior, as did the dome's thirty-two stained-glass windows, each emblazoned with the coat of arms of the Union or one of the states. A breathtaking 100 feet

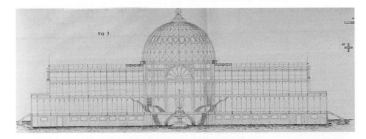

[FIGURE 1.12] The New York Crystal Palace, by Carstensen and Gildemeister. This is a section of the original design, adopted in 1852. Note the grand staircases leading from the first floor to the basement, the large central fountain, and the entrance next to the Croton Reservoir on the right-hand side—none of which was ever built. (Carstensen and Gildemeister, *New York Crystal Palace: Illustrated Description*,1854. Courtesy of Columbia University Libraries.)

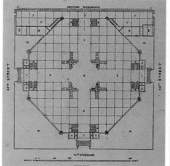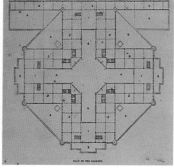

[FIGURE 1.13a and b] Plans of main floor (left) and galleries (right). By the time these drawings were published, the basement had been scrapped and the entrance next to the Croton Reservoir had been replaced by the machine arcade and picture gallery. (*The World of Science, Art, and Industry, Illustrated from Examples in the New-York Exhibition, 1853–54*. Courtesy of Columbia University Libraries.)

across and 132 feet high, the dome would make the New York Crystal Palace taller than the Crystal Palace in Hyde Park as well as the Capitol in Washington. What Carstensen and Gildemeister had in mind, in fact, would be the largest man-made structure in the western hemisphere (Figure 1.14).

Because the square sloped down from east to west, they would first have to construct a two-foot-wide stone foundation wall that rose from ground level near the Reservoir to just over seven feet in height on the Sixth Avenue side of the Square. This foundation, plus freestanding interior piers of brick and stone, supported the floor joists as well as 190 slender cast-iron

NEW-YORK CRYSTAL PALACE—SECTION OF THE DOME

[FIGURE 1.14] Section of the dome showing the bracing and, on top, the lantern
or cupola. "To our untravelled countrymen it may be a instructive example
of the beauty and fine architectural effect of which this structure is capable."
(*The World of Science, Art, and Industry, Illustrated from Examples in the New-York
Exhibition, 1853–54*. Courtesy of Columbia University Libraries.)

columns bolted to heavy baseplates. As in Paxton's Crystal Palace, the exterior columns were cast hollow to carry rainwater from the roof. Two hundred fifty-two horizontal trussed girders, made of cast iron and each roughly twenty-six feet long, would then be hoisted up by derricks and bolted to the vertical columns with special "connecting pieces" to provide the necessary lateral rigidity (Figure 1.15); another dozen girders, each forty feet long and made of wrought iron (a stronger material than cast iron), spanned the naves. These girders in turn would carry the floors of the second-story galleries and another 148 columns for the arched roof of the naves, maximizing the natural light reaching the interior. Forty-foot-wide fanlights would cap the ends of the naves. Four triangular sheds or lean-tos filled the spaces between the naves, creating the octagonal plan of the ground floor. At each corner of the octagon the architects placed a 75-foot-tall tower, inside each of which a circular stairway led up to a small observation deck.

Beneath the dome, multiple broad staircases connected the main floor with the galleries above and the basement below. The basement was an ideal space to exhibit heavy equipment like locomotives. The galleries, in addition to the usual "flower decorations, statues, vases, etc.," had space for a "Ladies' refreshment saloon and private room." In the center of the main floor, directly under the dome, Carstensen and Gildemeister placed an ornate fountain encircled by "statues, niches for

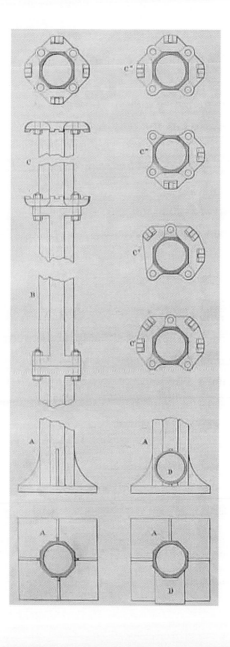

flowers, and other decorations, as well as tastefully arranged resting-places [that] will undoubtedly produce a very picturesque effect."

Altogether, the three levels of exhibition space—basement, main floor, galleries—comprised an area of a little over five acres, about one-fourth the size of the London Crystal Palace. The flooring throughout would consist of varnished pine planks. With the exception of the roof, which would be covered in tin, the exterior walls of the building—because they were not load bearing—could be made of nothing more than eighth-of-an-inch enameled glass fitted into wooden sashes. (Enameling made the glass translucent, not transparent, the idea being to reduce the heat and glare that had caused problems for Paxton.) The sashes were then to be mounted in the cast-iron panels of the frame (Figure 1.16). Outside, in a conscious attempt to replicate the countrified Hyde Park setting of Paxton's building (and to please local property owners), the

LEFT [FIGURE 1.15] Crucial to the construction of iron-frame buildings like the Crystal Palace was what Carstensen and Gildemeister called the "connecting piece"—a means of joining vertical columns to one or more horizontal girders similar to a modern portal brace. As shown in this drawing by the architects, the Crystal Palace required five different kinds of such connecting pieces. Each one needed to conform closely to specifications or the building would not fit together. As the Association noted, Paxton used the same method of construction for the London Crystal Palace. (Carstensen and Gildemeister, *New York Crystal Palace: Illustrated Description of the Building*. Courtesy of Columbia University Libraries.)

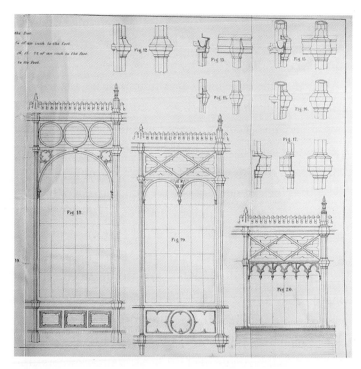

[FIGURE 1.16] Detail of the prefabricated cast-iron panels that formed the walls of the New York Crystal Palace. (*New York Crystal Palace: Illustrated Description of the Building*. Courtesy of Columbia University Libraries.)

architects proposed surrounding the Crystal Palace with walks and trees to create "an apparent artificial distance from the neighborhood," which "will be covered with houses very soon." As a result, boasted Carstensen, exaggerating only slightly, the aspect of such building will be entirely different from that of the London Crystal Palace: Its form affords all requisite scope for a pleasing variety of architectural embellishment, by which the monotony of Mr. PAXTON's design can be avoided, and allows a much more economical use of the given ground, which, being very limited, ought to be made as profitable as possible. The rising dome, independent of its effect in the interior arrangement of the edifice, will save it from appearing insignificant in the immediate vicinity of the Croton Reservoir; being higher, by ninety feet, than the latter, and contrasting favorably by the lightness of its style, as will the whole building, viewed near the massive walls of its heavy neighbor.[26]

Won over by the promise of a building more beautiful than Paxton's—and no doubt by the prospect of healthy profits in the bargain—the Association gave Carstensen and Gildemeister a contract in late August 1852. "A Crystal Palace on our own Hook!" exclaimed the *Times* when it heard the news. There could be no turning back now: "Private enterprise undertakes the financial responsibility, but the American people must face the music, or expect to be jeered by the London *Times*.... We might as well shave up, dress ourselves, and be prepared to make the best of it."[27]

TWO

An Honor to the Country

EVEN BEFORE FINALIZING its choice of architects, Sedgwick and the Crystal Palace Association got down to business. They started advertising nationally and organized a network of state committees to solicit exhibitors, reaching such far-away places as New Orleans, St. Louis, and Minneapolis. They hired a general agent to find European exhibitors. They arranged to have the Crystal Palace made a bonded warehouse so foreign artists and manufacturers could bring their goods into New York duty-free; later they would also arrange with the city to set up a private force of 100 uniformed policemen for security and crowd control (Figure 2.1). To oversee construction, they tapped Christian E. Detmold for the job of chief architect and engineer. The German-born Detmold was a hard-charging iron manufacturer and surveyor for the War Department known for (among other things) designing a locomotive powered by a horse on a treadmill. Capt. Samuel Francis Du Pont, a socially connected and decorated naval officer, veteran of the recent war with Mexico, and something of an expert on exhibitions, got the job of superintending the final organization and allocation of space in the Crystal Palace itself. His assistant, who came with a burgeoning reputation as an astronomer and editor of *American Ephemeris and Nautical Almanac,* was another naval officer, Lieutenant Charles Davis (Figure 2.2).

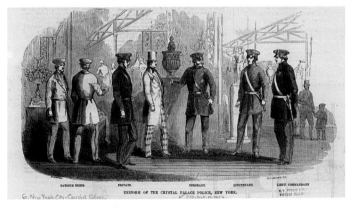

[FIGURE 2.1] The Crystal Palace police arresting a pickpocket. "The police of the Palace make no inconsiderable feature in the show, with their neat uniform, marked caps, and erect, gentlemanly bearing. They are well drilled and ready; but with an American crowd, largely composed of women, they have little strictly professional duty. But they have done important service in one direction, by showing, on a small scale, the value of a uniform dress for functionaries whose official character is their strength" (*Putnam's Monthly* 2 (Dec. 1853) 585). (Image courtesy of the New York Public Library)

[FIGURE 2.2 a and b] (left) Samuel Francis Du Pont, superintendent of the Crystal Palace and (right) Du Pont's assistant, Charles Davis. In its July 13, 1853, number, the *Times* praised the pair for "the discipline and skill which have presided over every aspect of the arrangements." It called both men "thoroughly accomplished scholars and gentlemen—prompt, courteous and energetic in every movement." In the Civil War, as a member of the Blockade Strategy Board, Du Pont helped plan naval operations against the confederacy but left the service in 1863 after he was unfairly blamed for the disastrous ironclad attack on Charleston. Davis, too, would sit on the Blockade Board, the first time he had worked with his friend Du Pont since their Crystal Palace days. (Courtesy of the Library of Congress)

Sheds for tools and offices seemed to sprout overnight on Reservoir Square, and within a month after the Association accepted the plan drawn up by Carstensen and Gildemeister, masons broke ground for the foundation. Contracts went out for 1,800 tons of iron columns and beams and 15,000 panes of glass, along with 750,000 board feet of wood and other material, which began to pile up on the square, contributing to the appearance of progress (Figure 2.3).

At the end of October 1852, workmen raised the first column into place while the governor, the mayor, Sedgwick, and a gaggle of other dignitaries looked on approvingly and nattered about great things to come. Some 2,000 people observed the proceedings, many from atop the ramparts of the Croton Reservoir, a popular vantage point overlooking the construction

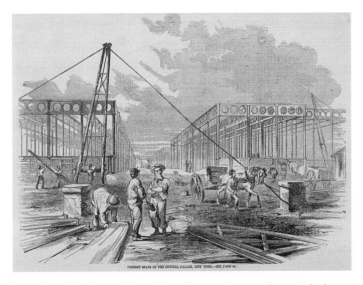

[FIGURE 2.3] Cast iron girders are hoisted into position atop the vertical columns using shear legs and pulleys. A pair of guys anchors the shears to masonry piers. This method of construction eliminates the need for scaffolding and was, until now, seen primarily in shipyards. (Courtesy of Museum of the City of New York)

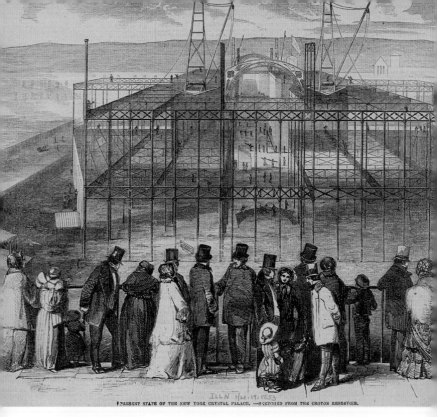

PRESENT STATE OF THE NEW YORK CRYSTAL PALACE. —SKETCHED FROM THE CROTON RESERVOIR.

[FIGURE 2.4] Reservoir Square, looking west from atop the Croton Reservoir with the Hudson River in the background. This view was published in the March 19, 1853, issue of Barnum's short-lived *Illustrated News* of New York. (Image courtesy of the New York Public Library)

site (Figure 2.4). Everyone cheered while cannons boomed and Dodsworth's Band "played delightfully."[1]

Construction on Reservoir Square continued throughout the winter and following spring. It made an impressive spectacle, by all accounts, with hundreds of men at a time "crawling

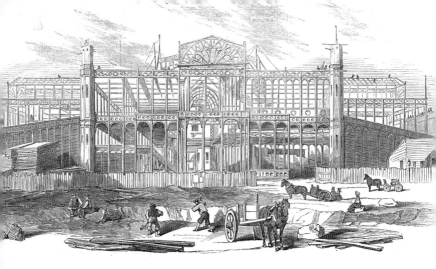

[FIGURE 2.5] Crystal Palace construction site looking east from Sixth Avenue. In this view, the framing of the building appears to be nearing completion and elements of the facade are visible. (Courtesy of Alamy)

like flies over the huge dome, men hanging like spiders from the lantern, men on scaffolding putting in glass, men inside making the galleries and laying the floors"—all scrutinized by the crowds that came up every day to this "newly-discovered Sedgwickian center of the metropolis" (in the happy phrase of journalist George "Gaslight" Foster) just to see how the building was coming along (Figures 2.5–2.7).[2]

Real estate speculators were hard at work, too, triggering a minor boom in the neighborhood. Weedy lots, neglected for years, suddenly fetched astronomical prices, and excavations seemed to be under way everywhere. Rumors flew (for a time) that the great Franconi would build his Hippodrome somewhere in the vicinity. The Brooklyn *Eagle* marveled at the way

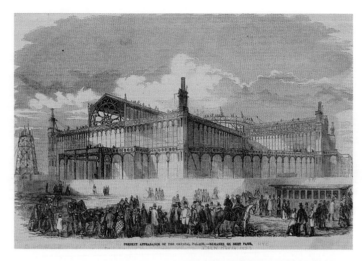

[FIGURE 2.6] The crowd watching work begin on the dome. Note that construction has also started on the Latting Observatory, which dates this view in the late spring of 1853. (Courtesy of the New York Public Library)

"buildings are going up like magic in the vicinity of the Crystal Palace... and enormous rents were demanded for mere shells. A room in one of the wooden buildings, opposite the Palace... was rented at *thirty-five hundred dollars per year.*" An especially enterprising fellow advertised in the *Tribune* that he envisioned "a first-class Hotel... fronting the Crystal Palace, to be erected complete by the first day of June next, on the south-east corner of 40th St. and 6th-Avenue. The building will be... five stories high, and replete with every modern improvement." He would be willing to rent it immediately, in advance of construction.

[FIGURE 2.7] The dome under construction, towering over the Reservoir "Workmen perched, like autumnal pigeons on leafy boughs, clustered within and without the vast edifice," gushed Horace Greeley, "and the magic web of improvement each day proceeded" (Greeley, *Art and Industry*, 16). As it neared completion, the *Times* likewise reported that "Scores of men, seemingly no larger than mice, hung pendant from the lofty and magnificent dome, coating its inner surface with the destined decorations" (*New-York Daily Times*, Jul. 13, 1853). (Image courtesy of Alamy)

Opinions differed as to whether this free-for-all was a blessing or a curse. The *Home Journal* was happy to find, directly across Sixth Avenue from Reservoir Square, "a new and really splendid icecreamery [sic] and restaurant, in which 800 people can be accommodated, with arm-chairs, at marble tables, at one time." Even before opening day, visitors could expect all kinds of exotic sights within a few blocks of the Crystal Palace:

living crocodiles, mammouth [sic] oxen, the model of San Francisco, the Swiss bell-ringers, and many others. There are plenty of men with targets and percussion guns, weighing machines and telescopes. Bowling saloons are numerous; so are swings, whirligigs and contrivances for wheeling people up half a hundred feet into the air. The cake and apple stands are past counting.

The *Times*, on the other hand, expressed misgivings about the increasingly seedy appearance of the area. "Wooden houses—many of them very frail-looking structures—are running up for the accommodation of visitors, and as temporary stores," the paper observed. "For the latter as much as $200 per week has been demanded in advance." In fact, everything thereabouts seemed to be made of crystal: "There are Crystal Stables, and Crystal Cake Shops, and Crystal Groggeries, and Crystal ice-cream Saloons. One old woman has set up a Crystal Fruit Stall, at which oranges and bananas, in every stage of decomposition, may be purchased. We noticed a dilapidated hovel on Sixth-Avenue, which was called by its proprietor the Crystal Hall of Pleasure." (The area's "vacant lots, rocks, and deep pits, with relics of country shanties" have nothing else to offer, the paper conceded on another occasion.) The *Constitution* of Middletown, Connecticut, warned innocent country folk to avoid "the hosts of liquor shops and places of low amusements in the neighborhood" of the Crystal Palace, which had spoiled whatever benefit the nation stood to gain from it. "They occupy the whole of the streets on two sides of the Palace, where they are arranged in long rows.…" Why the city's Common Council didn't do something about this unsightly carnival was a mystery. But the influence of what *Scientific American* called "crystalization" wasn't confined to the blocks around Reservoir Square. The Crystal Stables had recently opened downtown, it remarked, as had the Crystal Bakery. "And on the docks the other day we had an opportunity of drinking 'Crystal Palace ice-cool lemonade—one cent a glass.'"[3]

Around the end of the year, thanks to the diligence of the Association's agent abroad, the first foreign exhibits began to arrive—"flowing in daily," said the *Tribune*—from all corners of Europe. The sultan of Constantinople pledged to send exhibits from his country, "some very fine plaster casts of antique and modern statues" were expected any day from Germany, and so on. The Association meanwhile continued to stoke curiosity about the event with a national appeal for exhibitors, vowing that the Crystal Palace would be "the largest and most beautiful edifice in the country"—a boast that in the months to come would be spread far and wide by New York editors and publishers. Their message even found its way deep into remotest Minnesota, in mail carried twice a month over frozen rivers by pony-sled, emboldening a St. Paul booster named William Le Duc to wrest $300 from the territorial legislature to mount an exhibit in New York.

BUILDING FOR THE EXHIBITION OF THE INDUSTRY OF ALL NATIONS, AT NEW YORK.—(SEE PAGE 342.)

[FIGURE 2.8] On the first page of its October 23, 1852, issue, *Scientific American* published this view of the Crystal Palace from Sixth Avenue, commissioned at "great expense," and offered copies for sale at $10 apiece. It depicted the building with remarkable accuracy before construction had even begun. The Crystal Palace Association probably had its own official view of the building, because only weeks later, at the ceremony for the raising of the first column, the superintending engineer handed out a "beautifully executed lithographic representation of the building as it will appear when finished" (*New-York Daily Times*, Nov. 1, 1852). On November 23, the *Daily Times* reported that this lithograph had been widely reprinted in the American and foreign press. (Courtesy of the New York Public Library)

Scientific American, which had earlier raised a hue and cry against the Crystal Palace, now seemed to come around, too, even scooping the Association with a "superb representation" of the building (Figures 2.8 and 2.9). The magazine still thought James Bogardus had the more desirable plan and that no one anywhere knew more about building with iron. Nonetheless, it reasoned, "since we are to have a World's Fair in New York next year, we now hope it will be an honor to our country....

[FIGURE 2.9] One of many versions of the *Scientific American*–conjectural view, embellished with crowds and traffic. When this version appeared, construction had only just begun. (Courtesy of the New York Public Library)

In fact we know the Exhibition will be a benefit to New York city." Such an event, the magazine said, is sure to attract a "whole army" of Americans as well as visitors from abroad, maybe even Queen Victoria herself![4]

Things did not go according to plan. Work on the Crystal Palace steamed ahead under a cloud of acrimony and wounded feelings, so dark at times that completion of the building must have seemed unlikely. Certainly it wasn't the smooth triumph of private enterprise and know-how that it is often said to have been—unlike its counterpart in London, which had a much easier career because, thanks to Prince Albert, it could always count on royal support.

To hear Carstensen and Gildemeister tell it, the trouble started almost the minute their plan was accepted, when the Board of the Association eliminated the building's basement in a foolish attempt to save money. Not only did this lower the entire structure by about six feet, accentuating the bulk of the Reservoir in the background, but Detmold then realized he had nowhere to store heavy equipment or to display paintings. So they had to replace the eastern-most entrance with an "unsightly" two-story addition, right next to the reservoir wall and some 450 feet in length. This caused "serious injury to the symmetry of the principal edifice." Scrapping the basement also reduced the total exhibition space by 150,000 square feet, almost 3½ acres, leaving only a little more than 5½ acres. (By comparison, Paxton's Crystal palace boasted fully 16 acres of exhibition space.)[5]

The man in charge of the machinery department then discovered that an important beam engine would not fit in the new addition, so its roof had to be raised at the last minute, wasting more time and money as well as doing further damage to the overall appearance of the building. None of this would have happened, Carstensen and Gildemeister claimed, if the directors of the Association had stuck to the original plan—or at the very least not waited until the last minute to make up their

[FIGURE 2.10] Underneath the great dome. ("The American Crystal Palace."
The Illustrated Magazine of Art 2, no. 10 (1853): 250-64. *JSTOR*.)

minds about modifications. With the basement gone, moreover, they had to scrap the fountain under the dome. In its place they decided to put a huge equestrian statue of Washington by Carlo Marcochetti that the cognoscenti greeted with howls of derision exceeded only by their contempt for a nearby statue of Daniel Webster (Figures 2.10–2.12). Happily, nothing came of misguided suggestions to remove the second-story galleries and replace the dome with an open-air court.

Fearing that no one source could fill all its orders alone, the Board also let contracts for iron beams and castings to over two dozen shops in states as far away as Delaware when only one or two nearby would have been more easily managed (Paxton had only a single firm to work with). In addition, the foundries immediately jacked up their prices, forcing the Association to spend time renegotiating all the contracts. The roof leaked, too, because the Board ignored the initial design for gutters and louvers. It allowed Detmold to waste a couple of months experimenting with "some novel ideas" for the construction of the dome; at one point he even entertained the embarrassing idea of having the dome built in England! When it came time to decorate, the Board ignored the wishes of the architects and turned the job over to one Henry Greenough, brother of the late sculptor Horatio Greenough. Employing platoons of painters who spoke only Italian, Greenough made key decisions about color and other matters that risked "the destruction of all beauty in the building"—painting the inside

[FIGURE 2.11] Marcochetti's much-maligned equestrian statue of Washington, made of plaster painted to look like bronze. "It is bad," scoffed the *Tribune*. "It is beneath mediocrity…a colossal abortion…a bag of meal on horseback." It didn't help that Marcochetti used the same horse for a statue of Richard the Lionhearted previously shown at the Crystal Palace in London and now standing outside the houses of Parliament. Happily, the reorganization of 1854 saw the statue removed from its pace of honor under the dome and banished to the east nave. Four years later, following its destruction in the 1858 fire, the *Times* noted, "no one is sorry. An impossible horse, best ridden by an impassive clod, was not an agreeable object." (Greeley, *Art and Industry*, 55–56; *New-York Daily Times*, Oct. 7, 1858. Also, Goodrich, *Science and Mechanism*, 255; and Silliman and Goodrich, *Illustrated Record*, 52, 62.) (Image: *The World of Science, Art, and Industry, Illustrated from Examples in the New-York Exhibition, 1853–54*. Courtesy of Columbia University Libraries.)

STATUE OF DANIEL WEBSTER, ON EXHIBITION AT THE CRYSTAL PALACE, NEW YORK.

[FIGURE 2.12] John Edward Carew's *Webster*. "Absolutely, this statue is a disgrace to its maker, and an outrage on the memory of its subject.... We do not believe there is in town a wood-carver, who cuts figure-heads for ships, who would not lose all his customers if he supplied them with such work as this" (Greeley, *Art and Industry*, 56). "Probably the worst thing in the Exhibition," agreed Goodrich (*Science and Mechanism*, 255). (Image courtesy of the New York Public Library)

of the dome yellow instead of blue with red and white stripes, for example, causing it to appear one-third smaller than it was.[6]

To make matters worse, the Board failed to establish clear lines of responsibility and authority, so that Carstensen and Gildemeister "frequently clashed" with engineer Detmold and had to do the work of others:

> We superintended the surveying of the ground, the excavation for the foundation, and the foundation-work itself. We also inspected the execution of the work in the pattern shop and the iron-works.... At the same time we had to furnish working drawings for every detail of the construction.... We absolutely assumed the duties of the working officials in addition to our own, and superintended portions of the enterprise...we had not contemplated as devolving upon us.

Hardest to bear was a whispering campaign to the effect that the architects alone were to blame for what *Harper's* called "numerous and vexatious delays." Like Paxton, the two men should have "stood honored before the world...as the leaders and executors of a great enterprise," only someone—they weren't naming names but almost certainly meant Detmold—was conspiring to destroy them first:

> There was a steadiness and persistency about [these rumors]; a skillful and willful misrepresentation of motives, and

misstatement of facts, which rendered it evident at once that a secret and clandestine influence was being brought to bear against us. Numberless absurd rumors were set in motion, whispered from one to another, occasionally re-echoed by the press, and eventually, as is always the case, credited by many.

Their fee for so much trouble came to a modest $5,000—they suggested half in cash up front, half "as soon has the receipts of the Exhibition shall amount to 10 per cent of the cost of the building." The Association paid them $4,000. Of course, Carstensen and Gildemeister conceded, something will always fail to go as planned—problems must be expected in a project of such size and complexity—yet "whatever mistakes may have occurred during the erection, and in the completion of the Crystal Palace, they are not attributable to us."[7]

The Association had a different story, naturally. In their version, Carstensen and Gildemeister were uncooperative and touchy to the point of paranoia from the start. First, the two priced the Crystal Palace at $300,000—eventually it cost twice as much—knowing full well that the Association's charter limited what it could raise for the building to $200,000. Then they held up construction by arguing at every turn with Detmold about perfectly reasonable money-saving alterations. They didn't deliver the necessary working drawings and specifications when asked, embarrassing the Association and forcing it to push back the grand opening from March 15 to May 1, and then finally to mid-July 1853. Even at the last minute key elements still remained unfinished, however.[8]

At the end of November 1852—just a month after the first column had been raised on Reservoir Square—Sedgwick let it be known that the Association had probably made a mistake trying to do business with two relatively unknown characters in the first place (and a standard background check would have revealed that Carstensen had a history of quarreling with the Tivoli management until they decided to let him go). "When your plan was first submitted to us," he said in one of many irate letters, "you were all but total strangers to the members of the Board":

> one of you [Carstensen] just arrived in the country. You had for competitors, architects and mechanics of great reputation and influence, but the Board selected your plan on its own merits, without other recommendation or support, simply because they thought it the best, and because they believe that the beauty and originality of the design furnished proof that you fully appreciated the scheme and purposes of the Association, and gave an earnest of your future devotion to its cause. It is with deep pain that the Board find themselves mistaken in this just expectation.

The Board's dissatisfaction with their two architects became a matter of public record in the catalogue of the Exhibition, published in 1853, which lavished praise for the Crystal Palace on everyone *except* Carstensen and Gildemeister, whose names, tellingly, nowhere appeared in the text. Nor were the two recognized during the official opening-day ceremonies but sat anonymously in the audience. Horace Greeley was outraged by this "ignorant, stupid, vulgar" snub of the artists and mechanics who did all the work. "True to the barbarism of this country," he fumed, they were "thrust aside for epaulettes and white cravats." When the Crystal Palace in England was inaugurated, "the working-men who built and stocked the wonderful edifice, were kept like Roman slave-artists and laborers in the servile back-ground of swinish caste, yet there, even amid the shams of state, MR. PAXTON, the genius who waked it to life, was on the platform. But where we would ask, were the architects of our Palace, Mssrs. Carstensen and Gildermeister [sic]? Why were they not on the platform?" Where was Cyrus McCormick, the man whose reaping machine saved the country from disgrace in London?[9]

By 1855 Carstensen had gone back to Denmark, without either his wife or Gildemeister—ostensibly to work on a new amusement park because he had lost so much money on the Crystal Palace, yet doubtless happy as well to get away from all the unpleasantness in New York. Less than two years later, in January 1857, he died in Copenhagen, allegedly penniless and alone. Other than a few lines in *Scientific American*, the event passed unnoticed in the local papers. His wife, Mary Carstensen, did not remarry and remained in the city, perhaps with one or both of their two sons, until her death in 1880. Gildemeister stuck it out until 1857, when a financial panic and labor unrest ruined the architectural business, and he returned home to Bremen, Germany. His death there a dozen years later likewise went unremarked in New York. Engineer Detmold, the architects' nemesis, sailed for Europe soon after the Crystal Palace opened. He made a lot of money in coal, began collecting art, and settled in Paris. At some point he returned to New York, where he died in 1887. In his obituary, the *Times* called Detmold the "chief promoter" of the Crystal Palace and implied that it would not have survived "as great vicissitudes as have ever fallen to the lot of any similar undertaking" without him. The paper made no mention of either Carstensen or Gildemeister.[10]

-·●●●●·-

Everyone seemed to agree that the Crystal Palace would bring a flood of visitors to New York when it was ready, but when would it be ready? *Scientific American*, always glad to find fault with the Association, estimated that 100,000 people had come to town to witness the opening slated for May 1 (a wild exaggeration), but May became June and June became July, and still there was no word when the building would be done. When a violent hailstorm—the *Times* called it a "hurricane"—swept through the area on July 1, killing three workmen, smashing windows, and flooding the main exhibition floor, there was speculation that further delays would be needed for repairs. Crowds still came up to Reservoir Square to see how preparations were (or were not) moving along, although more and more of them also wanted to look at the unusual structure rising on the north side of 42nd Street, directly opposite the Crystal Palace. This was the Latting Observatory, the brainchild of a local inventor/hustler named Waring Latting.[11]

At some point toward the end of 1852 or the beginning of 1853, it had dawned on Latting that he could make money by charging people to climb hundreds of feet for a panoramic view of the city below, plus suburban towns and villages in New Jersey, Westchester, Queens, and Brooklyn. He issued $150,000 worth of stock, formed a board of directors, and, not having any experience in construction himself, hired an architect to draw up some plans. They started work in March and finished at the end of June, apparently with none of the finger pointing and backstabbing going on across the street.

RIGHT [FIGURE 2.13] The Latting Observatory, with the 42nd Street entrance to the Crystal Palace is on the far right. (Courtesy of the New York Public Library)

LATTING OBSERVATORY.

East side 6th ave 43-44 st burned 1858

[FIGURE 2.14] The Latting Observatory was a purely private undertaking. But it appears so often in pictures of the Crystal Palace that it is frequently mistaken for a part of the New York Exhibition. (Courtesy of the New York Public Library)

The completed Observatory was an octagonal tower, 75 feet in diameter at its base tapering to a mere 6 feet at the top (Figures 2.13–2.15), a dizzying 315 feet above ground—350 feet counting the flagpole, the equivalent of roughly twenty-seven stories—the tallest building in New York City, higher even than the spire of Trinity Church, over twice the height of the Crystal Palace, and almost certainly one of the tallest man-made structures in the world at the time. In fact, only the Great Pyramid of Giza (over 450 feet tall) and a couple of cathedrals in Europe were higher.[12]

[FIGURE 2.15] The Pylon and Perisphere, two of the most recognizable symbols of modernity at the 1939 World's Fair, appear here as reincarnations of the Latting Observatory and the Crystal Palace dome. (Koolhaus, Rem. *Delirious New York*)

Its frame consisted of eight timber spars bolted together and cross-braced, then secured to a stone foundation with iron straps. Patrons hiked to the top by means of a winding staircase, with several landings along the way to ensure "convenient opportunities for rest." (The original plan called for a central shaft or "well" to be used by a steam-powered passenger elevator, which would have qualified as a revolutionary innovation had it ever been installed. It wasn't.) On the uppermost landing, the directors of the observatory promised to mount an "immense" Drummond, or calcium, light "of sufficient power to light up the harbor of New-York," plus "a monster telescope" said to show objects up to sixty miles away. Entering or exiting, moreover, everyone had to pass through a long, two-story annex containing shops and an ice cream parlor, as well as "dissolving views, cosmoramas, scientific and optical instruments, works of art, and many other objects, useful and attractive."[13]

Lithographed bird's-eye views of cities were ubiquitous by the mid-19th century, but (like that engraving of the Crystal Palace published by *Scientific American*) they were relatively expensive. They were also inherently imaginary—the artist's *conjecture* about how the complicated landscape of a modern metropolis would look from high up in the air—typically enlarging significant buildings or geographical features to make sure the viewer grasped their location and importance. But a trek up Latting's Observatory democratized the bird's-eye view, so to speak. It was an invitation for anyone willing to pay the price of admission to see for themselves, fully and realistically, what had until now had been sheer speculation on the part of a few: the widening urban environment as it actually was (Figures 2.16–2.19). It could be an exhilarating experience, too, as a contributor to the *Home Journal* was surprised to discover:

> To tell the truth, we have been in the habit of regarding the building of this tower as a somewhat mad and Babel-like enterprise. But when, at the close of very hot day last week, we

[FIGURE 2.16] The Crystal Palace and Latting Observatory, a calotype by Victor Prevost. It was probably made in late 1853, after Prevost returned to New York from Paris in September of that year but before the dome was finished. (Courtesy of the New-York Historical Society)

had panted up its innumerable winding stairs, and stood on the highest of its platforms, inhaling the most delicious of cool breezes, and looked round at the varied and gorgeous panorama that lay spread out like an immeasurable carpet at our feet, we then blessed the name of our Latting, and extolled his tower as a wise, timely and beneficent institution. The entire geography of this region lies there magnificently

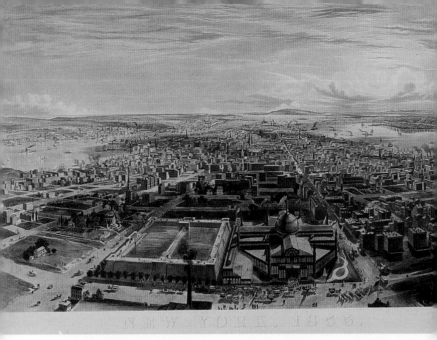

NEW YORK, 1855.

[FIGURE 2.17] "New York City from the Latting Observatory," by Benjamin Franklin Smith Jr., 1855. Unlike most bird's-eye views, this one shows the city from its relatively undeveloped northern outskirts looking south, rather than looking north from the Battery. The conspicuous curvilinear distortion of 42nd Street in the foreground suggests that Smith used a camera obscura of some kind, perhaps one equipped with a wide-angle lens. It does not, in any event, do justice to the striking appearance of the Crystal Palace. The official catalogue of the Exhibition said the exterior of that building was painted a "light-colored bronze," while "all features purely ornamental are of gold." (Courtesy of the New York Public Library)

mapped. The rivers wind about, and stretch away in broad lines of silver. Their banks are done in emerald and gold. The cities—New York, Brooklyn, and the rest—are painted with faultless accuracy. The spectacle is interesting and splendid in the extreme, and richly repays the fatigue of going up such a multitude of steps.[14]

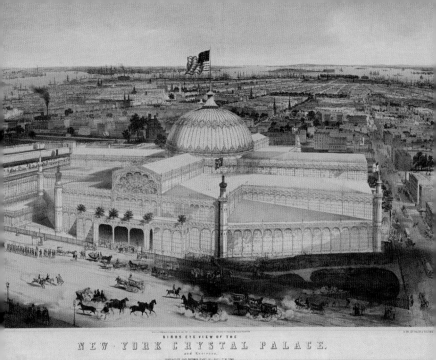

BIRDS EYE VIEW OF THE
and Environs.

NEW YORK CRYSTAL PALACE.

[FIGURE 2.18] A careful comparison of this view with the previous one suggests that this bird's-eye view was *not* from the Latting Observatory, despite striking similarities. The wide circulation of such images was unprecedented and helped build a national audience for the Crystal Palace Exhibition. "You may see the Palace lithographed, painted, engraved, and daguerreotyped in all the styles and sizes," said *Scientific American* in its Aug. 27, 1853, issue. (Courtesy of the Museum of the City of New York)

"The ascent is a little fatiguing," agreed the *Times*, "but it improves digestion." The City Council was equally impressed and only narrowly defeated a measure giving Latting permission to build a 600-foot tower to be called the Washington Monument next to Castle Garden on the Battery (one alderman

[FIGURE 2.19] The Crystal Palace from the northwest corner of Sixth Avenue and 42nd Street. The shacks on the corner are also visible in the view from Latting's Observatory. It isn't clear when this picture was taken, but inasmuch as the dome looks finished, it was probably in late 1853. (Avery Architectural & Fine Arts Library, Columbia University)

supported the idea because he thought the proposed monument was to rise directly *atop* Castle Garden).[15]

At last came the news that everyone had been waiting for and some probably thought they would never live to hear: the Exhibition of the Industry of All Nations, the first American world's fair, would open on the 14th of July, 1853. The Crystal Palace wasn't really ready, to be sure. The roof leaked, the dome still needed work, two-thirds of the exhibitors' stalls reputedly had yet to be completed, and the floors remained an impassable jumble of "quaint foreign looking packing cases, carpenters' tools, paint pots, half-opened bales, [and] vast derricks for uplifting heavy statues." Hundreds of men are working around the clock to get things ready, said the *Tribune*, and "the whole is a scene of exaggerated confusion."

On the bright side, New York teemed with excited visitors from all over the world. "It is the Exhibition summer," crowed the *Times*. "Everybody that is anybody is in town, and now is the time for meeting people in the streets." New York "is crowded and enlivened, as it has never been before.... The City swarms with strangers." *Harper's* observed approvingly that New York could boast of "more beards and barons; more Italian faces, and English plaids; more cosmopolitan talk and dress" since the Exhibition came to town, while a correspondent of *The Southern Literary Messenger* reported from New York that "the host of strangers with which the city is thronged" greatly exceeds the number of inhabitants "who are off on the fashionable summer tours, or sporting gay equipages at some renowned watering place, [which only] increases the prevailing enthusiasm, and gives a peculiar aspect to our over-crowded streets." Exclaimed *Putnam's Monthly*: the "grand convergence" of outsiders "makes our young city seem, for the time, a very London." And the traffic! "Hundreds of stages and cars, by their ensigns and banners," in the words of *Scientific American*, "proclaim that the Exhibition is the center of attraction."[16]

The shabby grog shops along Sixth Avenue had meanwhile taken steps to spruce up and offer new attractions. The *Times* reported that one, calling itself "The New-York Volunteers' Head-Quarters," was now "ominously surmounted by a huge representation of a crocodile destroying a riderless horse." Others were selling a novel concoction they called "root beer." Nearby, too, one of those machines had appeared on which, "for a very small consideration, you can suffer the same effects as arise from a sea voyage, by being propelled through the air in a circle of huge circumference." The canny proprietor had just "increased the number of cars for the convenience of the aerial voyagers."[17]

On the appointed day, people began to show up outside the Crystal Palace soon after sunrise, congregating in Sixth Avenue between 40th and 42nd Streets, directly across from Reservoir Square. The crowd grew steadily larger, hour after hour, fed by the arrival of overloaded omnibuses, stagecoaches, and street railway cars (Figures 2.20–2.22). Hackney cabs and private carriages, threading their way carefully through the milling throng, brought nabobs in top hats seated alongside ladies in colorful silk dresses. Bemused newspaper correspondents remarked on the large number of slack-jawed tourists and oddly

INAUGURATION OF THE CRYSTAL PALACE—INTERIOR OF SIXTH
AVENUE CAR.

[FIGURE 2.20] Straphangers on opening day, July 14, 1853. (Courtesy of the New
York Public Library)

INAUGURATION OF THE CRYSTAL PALACE—EXTERIOR OF SIXTH AVENUE CAR.

[FIGURE 2.21] The crowd begins to gather on Sixth Avenue. (Courtesy of the New York Public Library)

costumed foreigners, including groups of "very energetic Germans" and some "French gentlemen, invested in magical waistcoats." Eventually, according to information published in the *Times*, upwards of 50,000 people must have filled the avenue and nearby streets. Everyone was in high spirits, despite the congestion and muggy weather. Vendors of ice cream, apples, soda water, and other "curative agents" did a land-office business. Every groggery and eatery in the neighborhood was packed. The French girl sporting a beard and mustache, the mammoth ox, the five-legged calf, the two-headed pig, the

[FIGURE 2.22] Outside the ticket window of the Crystal Palace, July 14, 1853. (Art & Picture Collection, The New York Public Library, Astor, Lenox and Tilden Foundations)

lung-testing machine, and other curiosities on display in the sleazy midway around the Crystal Palace, as "numerous as the jubilee-days of the Champs Elysées," attracted mobs of "simple folk," Horace Greeley wrote in the *Tribune*. When the doors finally swung open at ten o'clock, lucky ticketholders, upwards of 20,000 strong, surged through the turnstiles (a feature borrowed from the London Crystal Palace) to wander the cavernous polychrome arcades, gawking at an extravaganza of machinery, sculpture, furniture, porcelain, firearms, antiquities, and agricultural products.[18]

Around two o'clock that afternoon, the sound of marching bands outside signaled the arrival of Frank Pierce, the New

Hampshire Democrat recently sworn in for his first and only term as president. Pierce had come up from the capital to preside over the opening-day ceremonies, landing at Castle Garden on the Battery that very morning and riding up Broadway on horseback, hatless, "erect as an Indian warrior." Throngs of cheering spectators slowed his progress, while a brief downpour left him soaked to the skin. By the time he reached Reservoir Square, the usually convivial Pierce, already suffering from a severe cold, was bedraggled and exhausted. He snagged a dry shirt from the owner of an ice cream shop near the Crystal Palace. Someone produced sandwiches and a flask of brandy, enabling him to take his place on the platform. With him came a crush of dignitaries that included several cabinet members (among them Secretary of War Jefferson Davis), two U.S. senators, three governors, assorted army and navy brass, a large number of clergymen, foreign ambassadors, and judges, along with three military bands, an organist, and a chorus (Figure 2.23). Bishop Wainwright led the multitudes in a prayer that seemed to go on forever, after which the Sacred Harmony Society sang a chorale written for the occasion by William Cullen Bryant.

When it came his turn to speak, Pierce took only a few minutes. He thanked the organizers of the Exhibition for their work, predicting that it would confirm science as the source of all "our domestic comforts and our universal prosperity" while it advanced the cause of world peace. Then, voice failing,

[FIGURE 2.23] Inauguration of the New York Crystal Palace—platform in the north nave—from a daguerreotype. (Art & Picture Collection, The New York Public Library, Astor, Lenox and Tilden Foundations)

he sat down. "The President is not one of your grave and earnest orators," one member of the audience conceded. Owing to the building's poor acoustics, only guests in the first few rows heard him anyway.

An organist played a march, a band followed with a waltz, "full of youth and love," and the Sacred Harmony Society closed the proceedings with an excerpt from Haydn's *Creation*. Pierce retreated to the Astor House, still the city's premier hotel, driven in a coach and six accompanied by Secretary Davis. The sun came out. That evening, at the new Metropolitan Hotel, the Association hosted a lavish banquet for the president and 600 guests. All in all, according to Greeley, the big event went off without a hitch—except that, once again, the architects received no more recognition "than if they had been two hod-carriers." Nevertheless, wrote the newspaperman, from start to finish, July 14, 1853, was a once-in-a-lifetime experience to be remembered forever as one of the great days in American history.

The *Times,* too, rhapsodized that the inauguration of the Crystal Palace in New York was certain to be "hallowed in American History as connected with an event of rare importance to the nation.... [The] sun of American industrial splendor which rose to-day, shall never set, but shine like the arctic luminary, ever above the horizon." Not everyone saw the future so clearly, to be sure. A correspondent of the London *Weekly News* thought the entire event vastly overrated. Everybody is talking about the New York Crystal Palace, he wrote—it is "*the* topic of the day"—and Americans brag so much about it one might think they, not Joseph Paxton, had invented the idea of building with iron and glass. But the sad truth is that as an exhibition of Industry and Art "it is a blank failure." The building is half empty and will display some rather "curious things," such as the 124-year-old slave who once belonged to George Washington. "What do you think of the showing up of a *slave* as an *article* of American manufacture?…*He is to be taken to the world's Fair for exhibition if arrangements can be made.*"[19]

·◦◉◉◉◦·

In its coverage of the opening-day ceremonies, the *Times* commented in passing that "iron construction on a large scale was and is entirely new in this country. No edifice entirely of iron yet existed in the United States, and the want of experience on the part of both architects and engineers presented serious obstacles." A couple of weeks later the paper published a rebuttal by James Bogardus, whose own plan for the New York Crystal Palace, it will be recalled, had been rejected by the Association. Actually, Bogardus explained to the *Times*, as far back as 1849 he had put up a factory "entirely of cast-iron" on the corner of Centre and Duane streets in downtown Manhattan.

A description and drawings of that structure had been published in London "before the London Crystal Palace was in contemplation," meaning that "it is not only the first building erected entirely of cast-iron, but the first in any part of the world."[20]

The *Times* was certainly incorrect that the New York Crystal Palace had been made *entirely* of iron. A principal reason it would go up in flames so quickly, after all, was the extensive use of wood for its floors, sashes, and dome. Nor was it the first building in the United States, or anywhere else, with a load-bearing iron skeleton. For decades already, British builders had been using cast-iron in mills, theaters, bridges, markets, cathedrals, train sheds, and houses—and selling prefabricated cast-iron modules to customers around the world. Even in the United States, the use of domestically manufactured iron columns, iron beams, and iron storefronts dates from the early 1800s. By 1853, cast-iron architecture was all the rage, and dozens of firms in New York and Brooklyn were reportedly experimenting with the commercial applications of iron construction. As *The Illustrated Record of the New York Exhibition of the Industry of All Nations* put it, "The use of cast-iron had … already become common here for warehouses, to a degree exceeding even its use elsewhere."[21]

Additionally, if the Crystal Palace wasn't the breakthrough the *Times* claimed it was, Bogardus himself may have misrepresented somewhat the construction of his factory on Centre and Duane, which some sources say was framed wholly or in part with timber. So the Crystal Palace doesn't necessarily qualify as the first all-iron building, either. Just about the only thing that seems beyond question is that nobody in America had previously attempted to build with iron *on such a large scale*—which is really what the *Times* had claimed in the first place.[22]

·⦾⦾⦾·

Judging by the fulsome praise it received around the country, in language strikingly like that used to describe Paxton's Crystal Palace in London, the New York Crystal Palace was an instant success—"a dream of beauty and utility never to be forgotten by those fortunate enough to see it," recalled a Minnesota businessman fifty years after he went all the way to New York from St. Paul to show off a birch-bark canoe made by Indians, an assortment of grains, and a live buffalo (which Sedgwick wouldn't allow in the building). Seventeen-year-old Sam Clemens, recently arrived from Hannibal, Missouri, told the folks back home that it looked like "a perfect fairy palace—beautiful beyond description" (Figure 2.24). The Crystal Palace "is an immense structure, of iron and glass," swooned the *Democratic Review*. It is "surmounted by a magnificent dome,

[FIGURE 2.24] Sam Clemens, in 1850, age 15, not long before he visited the Crystal Palace.

which glitters in the sun's rays, and is seen from some distance in approaching it on the avenue from below." The *National Magazine* described it as a "noble structure...the largest edifice ever put up in this country...an honor to the nation."

"The structure is very large," *Harper's* confirmed, "and architecturally is beyond all doubt one of the most strikingly beautiful fabrics ever erected in this country"—adding: "Seen at night, when it is illuminated by only thirty less than the number of burners that light the streets of New York, it is a scene more gorgeous and graceful than the imagination of Eastern storytellers saw (Figure 2.25)." The *Illustrated Magazine of Art* came up with the rather overwrought verdict that the Crystal Palace represented "a happy union of the airiness of tropical regions with the delicate, intellectual taste of a temperate climate." Among people who had seen both Crystal Palaces—among Americans anyway—the consensus was that the one in New York, though smaller, easily outshone the one in London. Enthralled, Horace Greeley wrote in the *Tribune*:

This edifice starts in its delicate beauty from the earth like the imagining of a happy vision. Viewed at a distance, its burnished dome resembles a half-disclosed balloon, as large as a cathedral, but light, brilliant, and seemingly ready to burst its band and stay aloft. In every sense, the Crystal Palace is admirable. To us on this side of the water it is original. Nothing like it in shape, material,

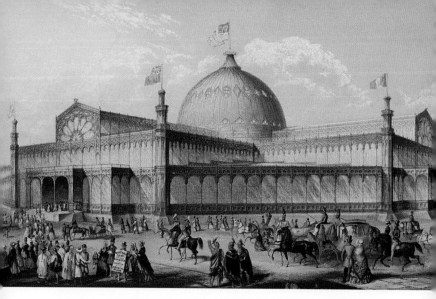

[FIGURE 2.25] It was often pointed out that the Crystal Palace eventually boasted almost as many gas lamps as the rest of the city combined. When the lights were turned on, the effect was magical. Said *Putnam's* with eerie prescience: "if the roof of the Palace were all of glass, the space it occupies would, at night, look from a distance, like a conflagration" (*Putnam's Monthly* 2 (Dec. 1853), 583). (Image: *New York Crystal Palace: Illustrated Description of the Building*. Courtesy of Columbia University Libraries.)

or effect has been presented to us. If it were to contain nothing it would alone be an absorbing attraction…. The brilliant and generally judicious coloring—on the insides as well as externally—of the glass and iron composing our palace, is a great improvement on the Quaker-like plainness of its London exemplar, which seemed but a paler reflection of those leaden British skies.[23]

Whether the Exhibition *inside* the Crystal Palace would inspire comparable adulation was the great unknown. If the stock market were any kind of barometer, it appeared that the months of delays and infighting had sapped investor confidence in the future. Prior to the opening, said the *Times*, the 4,000 shares of outstanding Association stock, initially offered at $100 per share, fetched $146—nearly 50 percent over par. After the opening, less than a week later, the price dropped to $125. By September, it had tumbled all the way to $77 and would almost certainly fall further. "But fortunately, the market value of the Stock affords no just criterion of the real value of the Exhibition," the paper hastened to point out:

> Its worth to the American people, and the degree to which they should cherish and use it, is to be found, not in the price of its stock when made the football of speculation, nor in the *per cent* of profit which it may return to those who brought it into existence,—but in the instruction it may convey to our mechanics and artisans,—to our farmers and laborers in every walk of life, and the impetus it may thereby give to those pursuits of Industry which constitute always and everywhere the elements of a people's growth.

Even so, all indications were that it might take weeks, even months, before anyone could fairly decide if the Exhibition as a whole had succeeded or not. Despite the official opening on July 14, the *Tribune* wrote, "The Exhibition is in a state which repels investigation and disarms criticism. It is a bird but half liberated from the shell." Week after week slipped by, and workmen still needed to finish setting up all the displays and getting a roof over the Machine Arcade and Picture Gallery. The Custom House had a large number of foreign consignments yet to process—everyone complained about lethargic customs officials—though more boxes and crates came in every day, obstructing the 40th Street entrance and blocking entire aisles inside. The refreshment saloons for ladies and gentlemen weren't open for business yet. Benches or chairs for weary visitors remained to be installed. Not until August 2 would the *Times* announce that "the Machine Arcade is beginning to assume form," although the steam engines that powered printing presses, looms, and other equipment still awaited necessary belts and pulleys. At last, too, "The Gentlemen's Refreshment Room is rapidly approaching completion, and the necessary conveniences for the accommodation of visitors are well advanced"—meaning the installation of newfangled water closets, a subject rarely mentioned in the press despite its importance to the comfort of the public. But not until the end of August, fully six weeks after President

RIGHT [FIGURE 2.26] Walt Whitman in his mid-30s, about the same time he visited the Crystal Palace. (frontispiece to *Leaves of Grass* (Brooklyn, 1856))

Pierce helped kick off the Exhibition, were they even prepared to turn the gaslights on. All things considered, the *Tribune* counseled, people should probably hold off visiting until further notice, especially "our Country friends."[24]

People came anyway. In droves—over a million of them before the Exhibition closed in 1854, according to the Association's own reckoning. Walt Whitman, a young poet from Brooklyn (Figure 2.26), came so often that the police grew suspicious and began to follow him around. Like every-one else, Whitman thought the Crystal Palace itself was "un-surpassed anywhere for beauty," especially at night, with the gaslights on. But nothing gripped his attention like *Christ and His Apostles*, a larger-than-life statuary group by the renowned Danish sculptor, Bertel Thorvaldsen (Figure 2.27). Among the most popular destinations in the Exhibition, Thorvaldsen's sculptures—"awful, grand and sublime," wrote John Reynolds, former governor of Illinois—always seemed to attract throngs of reverential visitors. Whitman himself said he spent many hours contemplating the scene. (There is no agreement, how-ever, as to what influence, if any, the Exhibition as a whole may have had on *Leaves of Grass,* the first edition of which ap-peared in 1855.)[25]

In his *Historic Tales of Olden Time* (1832), John Watson noted with sadness that recent advances in transportation like the steamboat and the Erie Canal had caused the "rage for

[FIGURE 2.27] *Christ and His Apostles*, by Thorwaldsen, the group that mesmerized Whitman. "Christian art has reached, in this immortal work…its noblest expression," wrote Silliman and Goodrich. "It is undoubtedly the great artistic feature of the Exhibition" (*The World of Science, Art, and Industry,* 51). (Image: *The World of Science, Art, and Industry, Illustrated from Examples in the New-York Exhibition, 1853–54.* Courtesy of Columbia University Libraries.)

traveling and public amusements" to begin trickling down from the fashionable classes to people who could ill afford either the time or expense. A creeping disdain for "good old house habits" threatened to undermine old-fashioned republican simplicity and frugality, for "where is the motive for patient industry and careful economy," he wondered, when everybody runs off for the summer to Niagara Falls, Lake George, Saratoga, Newport, or the beaches of Rockaway? Watson's darkest fears came to pass sooner than even he could imagine. A mere twenty years later, an English visitor could report that Americans had entirely succumbed to the "mania for travelling." Tourism had become big business for hoteliers, restaurateurs, and the publishers of maps and guidebooks— especially in New York, which seemed to empty out during July and August, when the *bon ton* and social climbers fled town for a country "vacation."[26]

Urban tourism, however—traveling to see New York City rather than passing through it en route to Niagara Falls or some such place "in the country"—was still in its infancy in the United States. Despite nearly two decades of prosperity and an epic demographic expansion that boosted the population of Manhattan past the half-million mark, not to mention a feverish construction boom that would soon enclose Reservoir Square itself within blocks of homes and businesses, New York before 1853 had nothing like the Crystal Palace to reel in sightseers—not the famously exhilarating crowds and traffic on Broadway, not Delmonico's or any other of the eating establishments called *restaurants*, not A. T. Stewart's Marble Palace (1846), a massive dry-goods emporium on Chambers Street often heralded as the first department store in the United States, not even the mammoth new luxury hotels like the Metropolitan (1852) and the St. Nicholas (1853), both built to accommodate the hordes expected to come to town for the Crystal Palace and among the first to boast of accommodations designed with entire families in mind—central heating, for example, or hot and cold running water in every room—plus that new lure for blushing brides, the garishly appointed honeymoon suite. Few if any would make a special trip just to see Barnum's Museum, the Custom House, City Hall, or the Merchants' Exchange, although locals held many of these places in high regard.

By and large, as always, most people came to New York on business, not for pleasure. Sadly, said *Putnam's* in early 1853, "New-York city is not wholly ideally magnificent." The work of lining her streets with "structures of stone and marble" worthy of a great metropolis is only just getting under way, "in spite of the mean and unsuitable docks and markets, the filthy streets, the farce of a half-fledged and inefficient police, and the miserably bad government, generally, of an unprincipled common-council, in the composition of which ignorance, selfishness, impudence, and greediness seem to have an equal share." At least respectable people tended to think that way. Waiting for the Crystal Palace to open, John Dalberg, the future Lord Acton, summarized prevailing opinion succinctly: "There is little to be seen in New York; it is not a fine city."[27]

Only after the Crystal Palace opened in 1853 would New York even start to look like a desirable place to visit in its own right. For thousands of Americans, as for the teenager from Hannibal, Missouri, or the businessman from St. Paul, the Crystal Palace was irresistible "destination architecture"—the modern miracle they had been reading about in the papers and now felt the urge to see for themselves. It would be difficult to exaggerate the breadth and depth of this feeling.

Popular journalists like "Gaslight" Foster recognized that strangers to the city were no longer just passing through. "Your chief motive, of course, in coming to New York at the present time," Foster said to his readers, "was to see the Crystal Palace." Not, he continued, "that you had any correct or decided idea as to what the Crystal Palace was or is—but that, as every body has been for some months past talking and writing about the Crystal Palace, and as you have been told that all the world is to be there, you naturally feel as though you ought to be there too; and so, here you are." The *Times* confirmed that the Crystal Palace "is much talked of in other parts of the

Union, and its opening will be the occasion of visits to New-York by many who would else have never trod the streets of the metropolis." Only a few years later, the same paper would credit the building on Reservoir Square with forever transforming the life of the city. "Until within a few years," it said, "New York was deserted in July and August, but ever since 1853, our great Crystal Palace year, our citizens have no sooner quitted us for their Summer excursions than a flood of country people rush in to supply their places.... The round of life in New-York is therefore eternal. When the City goes into the country, the country comes into the City."[28]

Increasingly, too, the idea that right-thinking republicans shouldn't save up for recreational travel carried less weight than it once did. To hear *Putnam's* tell it, Americans everywhere had been setting something aside for the trip to New York:

> Far back in the country, while yet the burning weather lasted, the thrill of this novelty was felt; in sober villages, in lonely farm-houses, in log-huts still haunted by deer and the prairie-wolf. Even then, preparations were making, excuses devised, and pence put by, for a visit to New-York as soon as the harvest should be housed and the heat abated. The Cryst*ial* [sic] Palace was the universal theme, the moment any one appeared who knew any thing about it.

The *Times* even hinted that travel wasn't a luxury any longer, and that people would be better off going to see the Crystal Palace rather than wasting their money on furs and the like:

> The Crystal Palace will draw hitherwards its thousands. Towns-people, too used to the shows and uses of this stirring world, know little of the eager anxiety of the rural districts to witness that novel assemblage of men and things. The money, which is to pay passages to New-York, and fill the tills of expectant inn-keepers, is stored away religiously in preparation for the day. The outlay is set down among the necessities of the year, not with the luxuries. There will be self-denial to procure it; fewer new coats, bonnets, furs, and Christmas gifts next Winter. All the roads, for a while at least, will lead to New-York. And all will be crowded.[29]

Around the same time, newspapers, magazines, and guide-books began encouraging people to think of the modern metropolis as an invention no less worthy of admiration than the steam engine or telegraph and to celebrate its creative energy as the perfect expression of American values. Increasingly, they emphasized the delights and benefits of city life, under-lining the profusion of commodities on display in New York's great stores and hotels and, by way of contrast, the hazards and poverty of the primeval wilderness. They began, too, writing about the city as no less picturesque or sublime than any natural marvel. It makes perfect sense that Latting's Observatory would be so closely identified with the Crystal Palace, because it helped promote the idea of the city as a vital and appealing component of the American landscape. "There can be no more lovely scene than is exhibited in looking down upon the city," said Humphrey Phelps in 1853, almost certainly from atop the Observatory:

> Broadway running through the centre of the city, lengthwise, a living panorama of modern and American enterprise; the Fifth avenue, lined for miles with princely mansions; the Bowery, and the various avenues cut at right angles by a hundred streets; the Battery; the Park; and the numerous public squares filled with trees and playing fountains; and the spacious harbors filled with ships, afford a picture the most beautiful and magnificent.[30]

Always to be kept in mind here is that a trip to see the Crystal Palace was, for the vast majority of Americans, a psychological as well as a financial hurdle. For the big city not only had more of everything than the village back home, it challenged visitors from the pre-metropolitan countryside with people and things that existed nowhere else—buildings of iron and glass, department stores, huge hotels, oyster cellars, and oddly costumed immigrants, to say nothing of the con artists, pickpockets, and other rascally characters from parts of town that decent folk should only read about in the papers. Danger lurked around every corner, not least of which was the dangers of *exposure*, of being recognized as one of those clueless out-of-towners, of becoming the butt of someone's joke.

A *Times* reporter, for example, told a story meant to poke fun at people ignorant of how things were done in the big city. It seems that one day in the summer of 1853, a couple of weeks after the official opening of the Crystal Palace, it rained heavily in New York until noon. Fewer people than usual ventured out to see the Exhibition, and those who did came encumbered with parasols, boots, and other foul-weather gear. Fortunately, to prevent them from poking wet umbrellas at, or dripping on, the displays, storage racks appeared at each entrance for their convenience. These racks "are attended by girls, who take charge of the articles deposited, and who give to visitors, in return, red checks, with printed numbers upon them corresponding to other numbers on the rack where the articles are placed." People in the know handed over their umbrellas willingly; others would have refused to comply, if not for the fact that "the girls in charge appeared somewhat strong-minded" and a few "imposing" police officers hovered nearby in case of trouble. And then there were those who just didn't grasp what was happening or what was expected of them. Serenely oblivious to modern city norms, they "thought the stands had articles for sale, and as the girls called out, 'Umbrellas, Sir,' replied with the utmost naiveté, 'Thank you, we're supplied.' "[31]

Anecdotes like that, told with a knowing wink, were not unusual in press coverage of the Exhibition, even in a place that otherwise welcomed visitors from remote parts of the country or abroad. Already, worldly-wise New Yorkers could not resist a good laugh at the expense of their naïve country cousins. Thus, just a week after the umbrella story appeared, the *Times* ran another account (perhaps by the same reporter) of "many faint-looking and wearied persons, looking sorrowfully around for some place to rest themselves." No sooner had these "unsuspecting sight-seers" settled into some cushiony lounge chairs than a policeman appeared and told them to move on. As sophisticated readers probably guessed right away, "the comfortable lounges were for exhibition, not for use." No doubt similar yarns were passed around about, say, the country bumpkins unaccustomed to the separate "retiring rooms" for ladies and gentlemen and their newfangled water closets—or at each entrance the "patent revolving registering gateway," i.e., turnstile, "an English contribution to the Fair," George Foster wrote, "an ingenious contrivance [but] unnecessarily clumsy and massive."[32]

·◦◦◉◦◦·

Not until the end of September 1853 was the mineralogical display ready for the general public, marking the de facto finish of construction eleven months after it began. Regrettably, a few exhibitors were already preparing to leave by the end of November, when they had been told the Crystal Palace would close for the winter. Instead of opening on May 1 and running for seven months as originally planned, in other words, the Exhibition had been fully operational for a little over two months, from late September through November. Hoping to recover their losses, the directors decided to stay open through the winter and brought in stoves. Now they proposed to keep going indefinitely. "The structure on Reservoir-square is universally conceded to be an ornament to the City," they said. "The trade and enterprise of New York, of its hotels, its retail dealers, the omnibus and railroad interests, have all been materially assisted by it."[33]

Scientific American, among others, wasn't having any. "This is not a satisfactory apology" for flagrant mismanagement, it fumed. The Crystal Palace had been drawing several thousand paying visitors daily since the early summer, or around $9,000 per week—less than expected, but no grounds for complaint. In truth, the Association wound up in the red only because the directors shoveled out cash and neglected the interests of everyone but themselves or their friends. Consider, the magazine said, the $10,000 they awarded to Riddle for the lease on Reservoir Square. Consider the princely commissions they paid to their agents at home and abroad, the thousands they spent to buy a copy of Thorvaldsen's group, the additional $10,000 they spent to buy Kiss's *Amazon*, another popular sculpture, or their purchase of an extravagant eleven-piece silver tea service as a parting gift for Capt. Du Pont, chief superintendent of the Exhibition. Consider, too, that the final cost of the Crystal Palace will probably exceed $600,000— three times the amount originally anticipated, equivalent to at least $13.9 million today. No surprise, then, that the Association went broke. Fortunately, the magazine concluded, an election of new officers would take place early the following spring, at which time Sedgwick and his boondoggling cronies could be replaced by more competent men—"men who will infuse a new spirit into the affairs of the Association for the benefit of exhibitors and shareholders."[34]

THREE

The Wilderness of Objects

BACK IN MARCH 1853, the directors of the Crystal Palace Association issued new guidelines for what kind of exhibits they hoped to attract. They began with the obligatory nod to the world's fair in Hyde Park two years earlier, calling it the "great prototype" for the one about to take place in New York. "It is generally acknowledged," they said, "that the London Exposition marks an era in the progress of the world—an era, of which the distinctive characteristics are the advance of those arts which increase the comforts and heighten the delights of life, the spread of amiable relations among rival countries, and, above all, the elevation of labor to its proper dignity." However, inasmuch as Paxton's Crystal Palace had contained numerous "objects of but little interest"—a criticism initially aimed at the American contributions in particular—the directors pledged to make "a more careful selection of articles" for the upcoming world's fair in New York. It would be inspired by its predecessor, but tidier, more focused.[1]

Only months later, the directors had quietly backed away from their promise of greater selectivity and restraint. Supervisor Du Pont announced that the New York Exhibition would use the same taxonomic system as the one used at the London show. This assigned each of some 4,300 exhibits—from 6,000 contributors representing twenty-three foreign countries—to one of thirty-one classes (Figure 3.1), with juries of experts to choose the best entry in each class. These classes ranged from "minerals" (Class 1) and "substances used as food" (Class 3), through "philosophical instruments" (Class 10) and "mixed fabrics" (Class 15), to "wearing apparel" (Class 20), "kitchen furniture" (Class 22), and "decorative furniture" (Class 26). The only differences between the two exhibitions would be that the Americans added a class for musical instruments (Class 30) and accepted paintings as one of the "fine arts" (Class 31)—no fewer than 675 paintings, in the end, hung in the second-floor gallery above the Machine Arcade.

Since everything on display was in some way the product of human industry, broadly construed, it became a challenge to imagine what would *not* qualify for inclusion. Among the 300 contributions from British Guiana, as a case in point, were

DIVISION INTO CLASSES.

All objects embraced in this Catalogue are separated into distinct classes, for the purpose of giving unity to the Exhibition, and to facilitate the adjustment of premiums and awards upon the final reports of the juries. With slight changes, the classification is the same as that adopted at the Great Exhibition in London, in 1851. A list of the classes is here subjoined:—

List of Classes into which articles are divided.

Class 1. Minerals, Mining and Metallurgy, and Geological Mining Plans and Sections.

" 2. Chemical and Pharmaceutical Products and Processes.

" 3. Substances used as Food.

" 4. Vegetable and Animal Substances employed in Manufactures.

" 5. Machines for direct use, including Steam, Hydraulic and Pneumatic Engines, and Railway and other Carriages.

" 6. Machinery and Tools for Manufacturing Purposes.

" 7. Civil Engineering, Architectural and Building Contrivances.

" 8. Naval Architecture, Military Engineering, Ordnance, Armor and Accoutrements.

" 9. Agricultural, Horticultural, and Dairy Implements and Machines.

" 10. Philosophical Instruments, and Products resulting from their use (e. g. Daguerreotypes, &c.), Maps and Charts, Horology, Surgical Instruments and Appliances.

" 11. Manufactures of Cotton.

" 12. " " Wool.

" 13. " " Silk.

" 14. " " Flax and Hemp.

" 15. Mixed Fabrics, Shawls, Vestings, &c.

" 16. Leather, Furs, and Hair, and their Manufactures.

" 17. Paper and Stationery, Types, Printing and Bookbinding.

" 18. Dyed and Printed Fabrics, shown as such.

" 19. Tapestry, including Carpets and Floor Cloths, Lace, Embroidery, Trimmings, and Fancy Needlework.

" 20. Wearing Apparel.

" 21. Cutlery and Edge Tools.

" 22. Iron, Brass, Pewter, and General Hardware, including Lamps, Chandeliers, and Kitchen Furniture.

" 23. Work in Precious Metals and their Imitations, Jewelry and other Personal Ornaments, Bronzes, and articles of Vertu generally.

" 24. Glass Manufactures.

" 25. Porcelain and other Ceramic Manufactures.

" 26. Decorative Furniture and Upholstery, including Papier-maché, Paper Hangings, and Japanned Goods.

" 27. Manufactures in Marble, Slate, and other Ornamental Stones, Cement, &c., for Construction and Decoration.

" 28. Manufactures from Animal and Vegetable Substances, not Woven or Felted, or otherwise specified.

" 29. Miscellaneous Manufactures and Small Wares, Perfumery, Confectionery, Toys, Taxidermy, &c.

" 30. Musical Instruments.

" 31. Fine Arts, Sculpture, Paintings, Engravings, &c.

"manufactures of the simple kind suggested by the wants of natives and the material at their hands," according to one report.

> There are bark canoes, bows and arrows, and war clubs, neck-laces, fans, calabashes, hammocks and mats of the palm-fibre, brooms, queus [sic], baskets, gongs, flutes, and shaak-shaaks. The three last-named articles are rude musical instruments with which the festivities of the Indians are enlightened. A dance without the shaak-shaak would be no dance at all. They resemble gourds, and contain seeds which make a great noise when shaken. The natives ornament them with feathers.[2]

As if to caution against drawing invidious comparisons between Guinean natives and the inhabitants of the so-called civilized nations, Class 3 of contributions from the United States—enumerated with a perfect lack of irony—comprised such products as "samples of fine tea in small packages," a "superior pine-apple cheese," "fine Havana segars," "an assortment of prepared chocolates," "a sheaf of wheat" from California, and "an article composed of pure milk and refined sugar,"

LEFT [FIGURE 3.1] Having criticized the London fair for exhibiting odds and ends, the Association adopted the same system of classification for the New York event—most likely thanks to supervisor Du Pont. Only the *addition* of a category for musical instruments was different. (*Official Catalogue of the New-York Exhibition*, New York, 1853)

among seventy-odd other items tenuously related at best to what ordinarily passes for manufacturing. Similarly, among the displays in Class 10—"philosophical instruments"—was a "Map of the United States" drawn by a student in the city's public schools, a skirt supporter for women, solid brass stomach pumps, and a "mechanical leech." Scattered throughout were doorbells, iceboxes, wigs, washboards, water closets, birdcages, fake diamonds, and silver sugar tongs. G. W. Tuttle, a local manufacturer of toys and other novelties, got up an exhibit of his wares. John Genin, proprietor of a fashionable hat-making establishment in the St. Nicholas Hotel, likewise assembled a "bazaar" showing off his new line off clothing and accessories for children.[3]

Instead of sharpening their focus, in other words, the directors had widened it or at least allowed it to become wider. Because this was still meant to be an exhibition of the *industry* of all nations, they intended to include "specimens of the industrial arts as shall generally interest the practical American mind." Even so, their latitudinarian notions of *industry* and *manufactures* had thrown open the doors to what Horace Greeley called a "startling array" of objects. "What is not there?" he wondered. It was not unusual, in fact, to come across visitors who were simply worn out trying to make sense of it all. "The mind becomes very quickly exhausted from the quantity of material crowded on the view," confessed a frazzled *Times* reporter, "and very soon produces additional physical lassitude. To-day we saw many faint-looking and wearied persons, looking sorrowfully around for some place to rest themselves." *Scientific American*, on the other hand, seemed to blame multitudes of childlike visitors themselves for the profusion of miscellaneous stuff in the Exhibition. "There are a great many 'curiosities' in the Palace," the magazine observed, "—enough to furnish a respectable museum, and about many of them, at any time, you may see admiring crowds of little folks, or of older people, who have come to see the marvellous. Anything very big, or very little, or very odd in any way, is looked at with the greatest wonderment and satisfaction."

One way or the other, declared *The Illustrated Magazine of Art*, people just wander around, "lost in an unprofitable stare, or an affectation of importance. The multiplicity and variety of objects confuse the mind." Truly, the Crystal Palace is "a wilderness of objects!" exclaimed a southern belle, giddy with fatigue. "Statues and statuettes, silks and satins, china and glass, furniture of all descriptions, and for all uses. What bright colors! what never ending glitter! What crowds of people. . . . Where shall the eye rest?" (Figures 3.2–3.3).[4]

Until the installation of gas lighting later that summer, the eye might well miss some objects simply because they couldn't be seen clearly. That proved especially true for items located on the east side of the building, trapped until afternoon in the

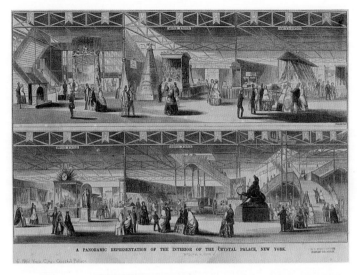

A PANORAMIC REPRESENTATION OF THE INTERIOR OF THE CRYSTAL PALACE, NEW YORK.

[FIGURE 3.2 a, b, c, and d] A panoramic view in four panels of the interior of the Crystal Palace, over the winter of 1853–54. (Courtesy of the New York Public Library)

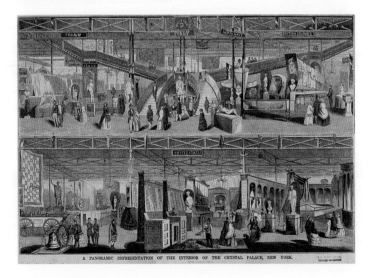

A PANORAMIC REPRESENTATION OF THE INTERIOR OF THE CRYSTAL PALACE, NEW YORK.

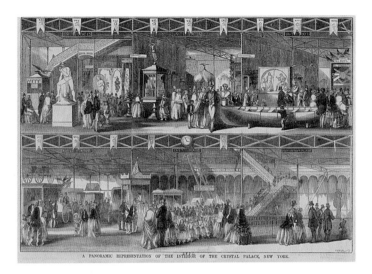

A PANORAMIC REPRESENTATION OF THE INTERIOR OF THE CRYSTAL PALACE, NEW YORK.

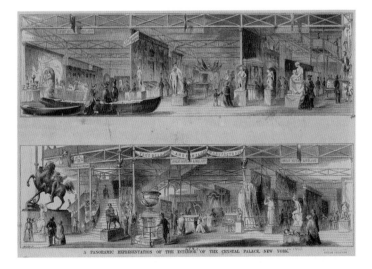

A PANORAMIC REPRESENTATION OF THE INTERIOR OF THE CRYSTAL PALACE, NEW YORK.

[FIGURE 3.3] Inside the Crystal Palace. (The Metropolitan Museum of Art, The Edward W. C. Arnold Collection of New York Prints, Maps and Pictures, Bequest of Edward W. C. Arnold, 1954)

shadow of the massive reservoir. Adding to this inconvenience, many things on display could not be clearly identified at all because no one was around to give explanations or answer questions. Frustrated by this apparent indifference to good public relations, Greeley's *Tribune* suggested replacing the policemen with informed docents—"men versed in the technicalities of each department."

Better labeling would have helped, too. "It seems to me extremely stupid in the greater number of exhibitors, that they expose their articles with so little explanation of their purpose, qualities and value," said the author of an indignant letter to the *Times*. "There is nothing to indicate to a visitor whether he is looking at a Reaping Machine or some contrivance to sweep the streets," the *Tribune* wrote irritably. "We heard the inquiry made fifty times while persons were looking at the most simple farm implement, such as a corn-sheller, 'What is this?'…Thousands of people will look upon these things who cannot tell a fanning-mill from a balloon, or a corn-sheller from a new patent rat-trap."

At risk, to the *Tribune's* way of thinking, was the educational mission of the Exhibition: people come to learn, yet they can't learn if they don't know what they're looking at. "It is a piece of excessive stupidity to send things here without having the name of every article just as plainly printed thereon as you are careful to have your own." Consider, said a reporter for the *Times*, the crowd recently huddled around an unlabeled object, solemnly debating whether they had found a fishnet or a strainer. Imagine their surprise when someone told them that it was only an Indian snowshoe![5]

In spite of these hurdles, *Putnam's Monthly* was pleased that so much evidence of practical American know-how could be found at the Crystal Palace. "In agricultural implements, in many kinds of machinery, and in cabinet and other woodwork," the magazine observed, "our working-men manifest an ingenuity and skill that will amaze those who have not before observed their products." This did not mean that things never before seen or dreamt of were on view. Except perhaps for the "electro-magnetic engine," a prototype battery-powered electric motor, or the "typeographer," an early version of the typewriter, visitors encountered very little that had not been unveiled previously somewhere else. The noteworthy thing, rather, was the sheer *range* of commodities already being made in the United States by machines—as well as the knowledge, so flattering to national pride, that Americans had invented the bulk of those machines.

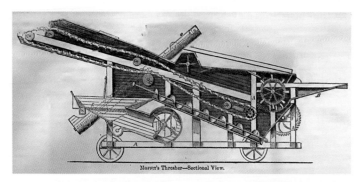

Moffit's Thresher—Sectional View.

[FIGURE 3.4] Improved grain thresher and separator, patented by John Moffit of Piqua, Ohio. A screw conveyed any unthreshed heads back into the machine. Like McCormick's celebrated mechanical reaper, Moffit's thresher was only one of dozens of ingenious labor-saving farm implements exhibited at the Crystal Palace. (Goodrich, *Science and Mechanism: Illustrated by Examples in the New York Exhibition, 1853–4*. Courtesy of University of California Libraries.)

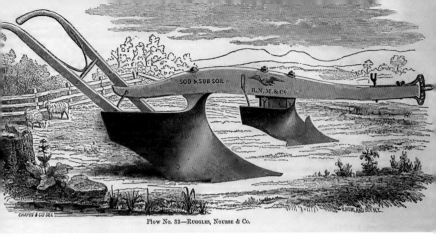

Plow No. 33—Ruggles, Nourse & Co.

[FIGURE 3.5] Sod and subsoil plow. Designed to bring fallow land into production, its two moldboards efficiently broke, flipped, and buried soil and weeds to a depth of ten inches. Many such plows were displayed in both London and New York, but this one, widely hailed as a triumph of American mechanical ingenuity, always seemed to draw a crowd. (Goodrich, *Science and Mechanism*, 130.) (Image: *Science and Mechanism: Illustrated by Examples in the New York Exhibition, 1853–4*. Courtesy of University of California Libraries.)

William Richards, author of *A Day in The New York Crystal Palace*, Putnam's handy abbreviated version of the official catalogue, steered fair-goers to some of the more remarkable of the many labor-saving devices on view, particularly in and around the Machine Arcade. There, Richards wrote, visitors will discover plows, threshers, ditch-diggers, road-scrapers, and other samples of prize-winning agricultural equipment (Figures 3.4 and 3.5) plus a fountain featuring a dome of water thrown over a dozen feet in the air by one of Gwynne's centrifugal pumps (Figure 3.6), a sheep-washing contrivance (without

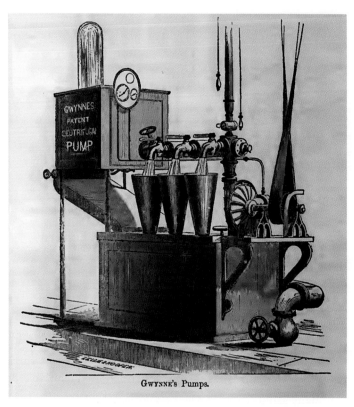

GWYNNE's Pumps.

[FIGURE 3.6] An American invention, manufactured in New York, Gwynne's centrifugal pump could move 1,000 gallons of water a minute or throw a column of water over 60 feet high. It was used to pump out mines and factories, drain swamps, supply water to cities for fighting fires as well as for human consumption, and other tasks essential to industrial development. In the Crystal Palace, one of Gwynne's devices powered a fountain in the east nave. (Goodrich, *Science and Mechanism*, 106; Richards, *A Day in the Crystal Palace*, 107, 114.) (Image: *Science and Mechanism: Illustrated by Examples in the New York Exhibition, 1853–4.* Courtesy of University of California Libraries.)

the sheep), and various machines for textile mills, including Eli Whitney's original cotton gin of 1793, brought to New York by his son.[6]

Near the south end of the Arcade, Richards continued, the objects displayed just outside the Ladies' Saloon "are rather important than attractive, and we pass stoves, and ranges, and boiler-flues, with a bare glance." East of the fountain, some visitors may want to pause to examine the sewing machines (Figure 3.7) or the two huge presses (Figure 3.8) used to print catalogues and other materials for the Exhibition. A "very ingenious" barrel-making machine deserved attention, too. It could cut and assemble staves automatically, even "heading and hooping them completely." Then there was the 30-horsepower Southern Belle , an engine "so elaborately finished that it cost $7,000." Flanking it, rigged so as to power machines in the Arcade, stood two huge 60-horsepower engines connected by underground pipes to boilers located across 42nd Street. "It is interesting," Richards mused, to watch these three powerful devices working side by side, "the huge flywheels revolving, levers and beams reciprocating with the very sublimest 'poetry of motion' our imagination can comprehend." And just beyond them loomed a "mammoth rock-drill—a vast steel augur propelled by steam, to bore holes in granite or other rocks, a striking exemplification of the *power* of machinery."[7]

SINGER's Sewing Machine.

[FIGURE 3.7] Of the ten sewing machines exhibited at the Crystal Palace, Isaac Singer's drew the most attention. His machine, patented in 1851, made 200 stitches per minute, compared to 40 for a fast seamstress, and employed an innovative foot treadle. It also borrowed features from prior inventors, among them Elias Howe, who sued Singer for copyright infringement and won. By 1856, this and other litigation between rival claimants had generated such acrimony (and expense) that Howe, Singer, and several others formed the Sewing Machine Combination to pool their patents and stabilize the market. In the same year, Singer began to sell smaller machines for home use, previous models having been intended for the manufacturers of clothing, shoes, and the like. (Goodrich, *Science and Mechanism*, 111; Silliman and Goodrich, *Science, Art, and Industry*, 6.) (Image: *Science and Mechanism: Illustrated by Examples in the New York Exhibition, 1853–4*. Courtesy of University of California Libraries.)

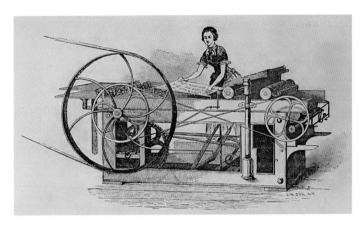

[FIGURE 3.8] The Adams Cylinder press. One of two working printing presses inside the Crystal Palace owned by G.P. Putnam & Co., the Exhibition's official publisher. It could be operated by one person, "usually a girl, whose duty it is to supply the sheets of paper one by one." The other was a platen or flat-plate Taylor press, slower but better for engravings and other fine work. (Silliman and Goodrich, *Science, Art, and Industry*, 87–88; Richards, *A Day in the Crystal Palace*, 109.) (Image: *Science and Mechanism: Illustrated by Examples in the New York Exhibition, 1853–4*. Courtesy of University of California Libraries.)

Just beyond various devices for sawing, planing, and mortising wood, "the careful housewife" would come across King's patented washing machine. This clever apparatus, consisting of a 20-gallon revolving tank, could clean sixty or seventy soiled garments in five minutes "without rubbing." Equipped with its own boiler for steam, it cost $75. Not far away stood Dick's boiler punch, "a powerful machine for punching holes in boiler iron," and next to it, a gold-beater's hammer, "with its everlasting trip, trip."

Contributing to the racket were dozens of pumps for every imaginable purpose (Figure 3.9). "From the little hand-pump to the formidable hydraulic ram, they are before us, spouting or pouring incessantly." In fact, the din in the Arcade must have

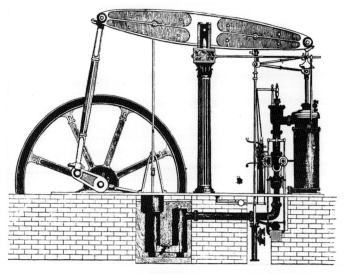

[FIGURE 3.9] Condensing beam engine, used in a Charleston, Virginia (now West Virginia), lead mine for pumping and to bring up ore. It boasted a 24-inch cylinder with a 5-foot stroke and could move 216 gallons of water a minute. An ingenious device similar to the float of a modern sump pump automated its operation. (Richards, *A Day in the Crystal Palace*, 110; Silliman and Goodrich, *Science, Art, and Industry*, 85.) (Image: *Science and Mechanism: Illustrated by Examples in the New York Exhibition, 1853–4.* Courtesy of University of California Libraries.)

seemed close to unbearable at times. At one point, Richards mischievously cautioned people with "weak nerves" to avoid the section reserved for textile manufacturing because of the noise. "Here are looms and spinners of every description," he explained, "and they whirl, and whiz, and thump, and bang, with delightful impunity."[8]

·=◦◊◦◊◦◦=·

Strictly speaking, this wilderness of objects was called the Exhibition of the Industry of All Nations, but from the beginning people sometimes referred to it as the Exhibition of the *Art* and Industry of All Nations. Greeley chose *Art and Industry* as the title for his collection of *Tribune* articles about the Crystal Palace. Likewise, when Silliman and Goodrich repackaged the individual numbers of *The Illustrated Record* as a single volume, they called it *The World of Science, Art, and Industry*. And, in the words of the *Tribune*: "The great utility of the Crystal Palace consists in its forming of a standard of Art, and an exchange for testing the values of Industry."[9]

Giving *Art* equal billing with *Industry* wasn't so much a mistake as a reflection of the fact that the exhibits of the fine arts (painting, sculpture, photography, architecture) and the decorative arts (ceramics, glassware, furniture, jewelry, textiles, woodwork) greatly outnumbered those devoted to machinery. Of the 504 woodcuts in the *Illustrated Record*, only

40 (8 percent) depicted machinery, while 371 (74 percent)—
nearly three-quarters of the total, representing more than
2,500 of 3,400 items—depicted sculpture, textiles, furniture,
porcelain, terra-cotta, glassware, and the like. No wonder visitors to the Crystal Palace often seemed unable to take it all in.
There was just too much stuff indirectly related, at best, to industrialization—a wide-open, dazzling, unforgettable extravaganza, albeit one that verged on overwhelming nevertheless.[10]

Like the original Crystal Palace in London, the one in New
York came freighted with heavy didactic purpose—less to
promote industrialization as such than to promote it by culti-
vating an appreciation for its best and most desirable products.
In their preface to *Science, Art, and Industry,* Silliman and
Goodrich promised to put forward "a correct appreciation of
what is really beautiful in the arts of design—to awaken in the
people of the United States a quicker sense of the grace and
elegance of which familiar objects are capable." Notwithstanding the great progress made in this area over the last
decade, they wrote, much remains to be done. "The public
mind is…moving in the right direction. It needs, however,
constant watchfulness to guard against the errors growing out
of a tendency to admire what is overwrought or extravagant,
and to substitute splendor of color, and costliness of material,
for beauty of form, and elegance of design." Only an expert
could keep up this "constant watchfulness," discriminating

between good design and bad, and it didn't take much imagination to figure out who they thought most likely to become an expert.

The crux of the matter, as Silliman and Goodrich saw it, was that "the masses in the United States have no knowledge of Art, for the plain reason that they have had no opportunity to instruct themselves in it." Unlike Europeans, Americans don't have sculpture, paintings, or antiquities to educate them, and only a comparative few enjoy the wealth and leisure necessary to travel abroad and experience art firsthand. This is not to say that the upper classes alone should acquire good taste. "To those who know the power of Art to educate and refine the taste, the social life and character of a people, it has always been a cause of regret that the appreciation and enjoyment out of it should have been confined to the few whose wealth was equal to purchase all of its costly productions."

Happily, at least on this side of the Atlantic, even the poor can appreciate beautiful things, given the chance. Excellent yet inexpensive reproductions of the best art today lie within reach of everyone, while exhibitions like the one at the Crystal Palace enable all classes to study "good models" of "sound taste." For only the refinement of taste—the cultivation of true *connoisseurship*, not merely "constructive or mechanical talent" alone—can advance manufacturing; as Silliman and Goodrich saw it, because visitors to the Crystal Palace were *consumers* as well as spectators, industry could not flourish without "a high standard of taste" among the poor as much as among the rich. Ideally, to that end, the Crystal Palace will inspire the American people to demand the creation of "museums of Antiquities and the Fine Arts, of Natural History, the Mechanical Arts and manufactures, in all our principal towns."

Old-fashioned ideas about the imperatives of republicanism, Silliman and Goodrich went on, "are yielding to a juster appreciation of the true place and uses of Art. We are no longer contented with the plainness that was once satisfactory. A demand for decoration has arisen in every branch of manufactures; and although ornament has sometimes been used to excess, and inappropriately, it is still a movement in the right direction, and shows the necessity of an art-education among the people by familiarity with the works of the best masters." To hone the connoisseurship of visitors to the Crystal Palace, Silliman and Goodrich loaded *Science, Art, and Industry* with helpful case studies of good art versus bad art—appropriate decoration versus excessive decoration—none more revealing than those involving household furniture.

Furniture could be found throughout the Crystal Palace and may well have been the single most commonly displayed item. By and large the examples came from the workshops of craftsmen in New York, Boston, and Philadelphia and generally involved the heavy, ornate tables, buffets, sideboards, armchairs, sofas, headboards, bookcases, and pianofortes currently in fashion among the nascent urban bourgeoisie (Figures 3.10 and 3.11). The ubiquitous buffets in particular did not speak well "of our good sense or our perceptions of beauty or fitness," Silliman and Goodrich wrote. Of necessity, "a buffet requires a large dining-room and a respectable display of plate; which requires a large and sumptuously furnished house; which requires a corresponding equipage retinue of servants." Many social-climbing city residents nevertheless boast of a buffet—without plate. "Preposterous fools!" Not a hundred private houses in the city have a dining room large enough for a genuine buffet, the two pointed out, and "certainly not that number the owners of which can afford to live in the style in which a man should live who has a buffet properly covered." Furniture makers won't stop producing these monstrosities until people of "frivolous and degraded taste" learn to stop buying them. A "more modest sideboard" (Figure 3.12) would be the better choice for most customers, Silliman and Goodrich believed, as it "can be made sufficiently beautiful and sufficiently costly to be a becoming decoration for any dining-room."[11]

But was this hankering for luxury—this *materialism*—consistent with our values and traditions? Once upon a time, Americans of all classes believed that Spartan frugality and

[FIGURE 3.10] A "truly magnificent buffet" made of American oak in New York. "One of the most noticeable objects that challenge the attention of the visitor to the Exhibition.... The ornaments are not only excellent and meritorious in themselves, but they have a characteristic significance in their application. They consist of representations of the game and fruits, which are disposed with judicious taste, and are relieved with decorations cut in geometric forms." It is very big, however, and "only fit for the dining-hall of a castle or a manor-house" (Silliman and Goodrich, *Science, Art, and Industry*, 168, 185). (Image: *Science and Mechanism: Illustrated by Examples in the New York Exhibition, 1853–4*. Courtesy of University of California Libraries.)

[FIGURE 3.11] Rosewood étagère, made in Brooklyn. "In the American department of the Exhibition, we have been agreeably surprised to find a number of pieces of ornamental furniture of large size, which, in design and elaborate and excellent workmanship . . . compare on equal terms with the production of foreign manufactories. . . . [The] fact that such costly and beautiful articles are executed at all, shows that there is a progressive development of taste in the minds of our citizens, corresponding to their increasing wealth" (Silliman and Goodrich, *Science, Art, and Industry*, 93). (Image: *Science and Mechanism: Illustrated by Examples in the New York Exhibition, 1853–4*. Courtesy of University of California Libraries.)

[FIGURE 3.12] Black walnut sideboard, made in New York. "The material is one admirably adapted to display this skill of the cabinet-maker and the carver, and the size is not too large for the use and style of moderately wealthy families" (Silliman and Goodrich, *Science, Art, and Industry*, 162–63). (Image: *Science and Mechanism: Illustrated by Examples in the New York Exhibition, 1853–4*. Courtesy of University of California Libraries.)

simplicity should be sufficient for a republican people. Even now, the Rev. Henry Bellows explained to his well-heeled congregation at the First Congregational (Unitarian) Church, the idea persists in some circles that luxury, like travel, corrodes virtue—that "multiplying and perfecting the comforts and elegancies of daily life" will drown us in "that indolent self indulgence, that soft effeminacy, that vicious materialism," which ruined older nations. Aristocratic ostentation is still inappropriate for Americans. But we should not equate luxury today with the "debilitating and demoralizing" luxury that afflicted England or France in the past because an appreciation of it is no longer just "the indulgence of a class." On the contrary, Bellows went on, here in America—the "destined home of universal comfort and splendor"—luxury has now been diffused through the entire population. It is eagerly sought by "large masses of our people," conscious that "comfort and elegance, instead of brutifying man, have a direct and powerful tendency to soften his heart, open his conscience, and refine his soul." After all, as everyone knows, "if you would give a man of rude manners some refinement, place him where every object he sees checks his boorishness. . . . The whole tendency of rude, ill-furnished, inelegant homes is to make or perpetuate within them rude, graceless and reckless occupants." There exists a direct correlation "between the development of the mind and the decencies of civilized life."

Instead of dismissing the Crystal Palace Exhibition as a danger, therefore, we should welcome it "as a great popular advertisement—a plan for letting the people know what is to be had, and who has it—a scheme for creating wants by exhibiting ingenious means of supplying them, and thus developing new forms of labor and new markets for them." The Crystal Palace would legitimize luxury.[12]

-··◦◦●●◦◦·-

One day before the official opening of the Crystal Palace, an essay in the *Tribune*, in all likelihood the work of Horace Greeley, went further than Bellows and suggested that exposing ordinary Americans to the arts and similar "refinements of wealth" would usher in a new era of social peace and harmony by quieting class resentment:

Mere wealth, without the refinements of wealth—barbaric ostentation, prodigal display, extravagant self-indulgence—can only corrupt morals and degrade character. But the cultivation of the finer arts redeems society of its grossness, spreads an unconscious moderation and charm around it, softens the asperities of human intercourse, elevates our ideals, and imparts a sense of serene enjoyment to all social relations. Our common people, immeasurably superior to the common people of other nations, in easy means of subsistence, in intelligence, as in the sterling virtues, are yet almost as immeasurably behind them in polished and gentle manners, and the love of music, painting, statuary, and all the more refining social pleasures.

True, Silliman and Goodrich acknowledged, the effect of good taste "is much too subtle to be exactly appreciated. It is not possible to determine just how much it benefits a man to see an exquisite vase, or to hear a fine strain of music, or contemplate a masterful statue. But it is very easy to perceive that he who is subject to the constant influence of beautiful forms is in a fair way to have beautiful feelings." And with those forms now available to everyone, no one had any excuse for boorish behavior.

As it happened, however, "beautiful feelings" between the classes were in short supply, especially in New York, during the booming 1850s. Few working people would likely have admitted to the "serene enjoyment" of their relations with those richer and more influential than themselves. The kind of men who, as the writer N. P. Willis described them, "keep carriages, live above Bleecker, are subscribers to the opera, go to Grace Church, have a town house and country house, give balls and parties"—men such as this spoke openly about the need to use force to suppress popular disorders, in America as well as in Europe, and wondered if warfare with the "dangerous classes" lay just around the corner. Some of this worrying was a reaction to the confrontational Young America movement and to John O'Sullivan's influential journal, *The Democratic Review,* which could whip itself into a lather of enthusiasm for almost anything that sounded youthful, fresh, or revolutionary. Some of this concern was triggered, too, by the popularity of egalitarian, anti-monopolistic, Locofoco, or Barnburner elements within the Democratic Party.[13]

At least in New York, most of this bourgeois anxiety stemmed from a succession of riots, brawls, strikes, and other public disturbances in the late 1840s and early 1850s. Prosperity for some, it seems, did not float all boats. The great Astor Place Riot of 1849—the worst example of urban disorder before the Draft Riots in 1863—saw the militia firing on a large crowd of workingmen outside the Opera House, many of them Irish, killing 22 and wounding 150. Evidently, according to one account of the affray, the "hatred of wealth and privilege is increasing over the world, and ready to burst out whenever there is the slightest occasion."

In the summer of 1850, a demonstration by German tailors escalated quickly to bloody brawls with the police, threats of a general strike, and progress toward the unity of everyone who labored for a wage, regardless of craft or ethnicity. Another battle with the police in August of that same year killed two tailors and left dozens wounded. A few months later, in early

October 1850, the city's African American population organized a mass interracial rally on behalf of James Hamlet, a free man seized by federal agents enforcing the new Fugitive Slave Act—perhaps the first time in the city's history that whites had turned out in such numbers for an event staged by blacks. In May 1851 one person was killed and many injured when German picnickers from New York City fought a pitched battle with Irish rowdies across the Hudson River in Hoboken, New Jersey. More recently, in December 1851, around the time planning got under way for a Crystal Palace in New York, delirious throngs greeted the Hungarian freedom fighter Louis Kossuth at Castle Garden.[14]

In 1852, Irish and German gangs clashed on numerous occasions with one another, with nativists, and with the police who tried to intervene, using bottles, bricks, paving stones, clubs, axes, shovels, knives, and guns. They bit off ears, broke noses, and gouged out eyes; fractured bones were routine, fatalities not uncommon. "Another Bloody Tragedy" exclaimed the *Times* in its description of the obviously pre-arranged melee between Irishmen and Germans in which one man died outright and seven others were not expected to survive their wounds. Almost every week that year seemed to bring news of brawling between rival gangs, brazen assaults in broad daylight, and shocking murders. Angry mobs attacked jails, Tammany headquarters, polling places, the Bowery Circus, and assorted saloons. Some "desperate negroes" assaulted German grocers near the Five Points slum, the *Times* reported with alarm. "It appears the black rogues have been in the habit of creating mobs and annoying the Germans without provocation."

That October, just as construction of the Crystal Palace got under way, the waterfront was convulsed for two weeks when caulkers, riggers, stevedores, and longshoremen walked off the job and paraded through the streets, "cotton hooks and sheath knives" tucked menacingly in their belts. With the port at a virtual standstill, incidents of violence were reported between the strikers and strikebreakers hired by the big importers. (The *Times* claimed that the "Shipping Riots" ended only when the mayor threatened to call out the militia and sent 500 policemen to patrol South Street. The *Tribune*, predictably somewhat more sympathetic to workingmen, called it the "Riggers' Strike" and said it ended when right-thinking employers agreed to give the men a raise.) At the end of the month, however, came the reassuring news that the city had built a new armory downtown on the corner of White and Elm streets. Its commodious second floor could be used for drilling or, "in case of riot," as a "rendezvous."[15]

In 1853 and 1854—coinciding almost exactly with the occupation of the Crystal Palace by the Exhibition of the Industry of All Nations—the dailies carried frequent reports of brawls between fire companies or gangs headquartered in the Five

Points. Rioting erupted in March 1853 when a streetcar inter-
rupted a funeral procession, in June when some children discovered a barrel of human bones hidden in a drugstore on 17th
Street, and again on Independence Day when a runaway horse
disrupted a parade of the Ancient Order of Hibernians. On
the latter occasion, two nearby fire companies joined the fray
on the side of the police, who arrested thirty-six Hibernians
before restoring order. That summer, rioting broke out aboard
a steamer returning from an excursion to Yonkers and when
police tried to arrest members of the Honeymoon Gang.

There was constant unrest in the East River shipyards, such
as the day in December 1853 that a notorious street preacher
was arrested for an inflammatory tirade against the Catholic
Church and a mob of 5,000 or 6,000 laborers from the waterfront threatened to burn down or blow up Mayor Westervelt's
house unless he released the man. A race riot outside an oyster
saloon left one man dead and several others not expected to
survive their wounds, one of them having been "cut and
carved about his face in a shocking manner."[16]

"Well-dressed, well-fed, jolly-countenanced men"—like
those in charge of the Exhibition—retired every night more
certain than the night before that things in New York were
getting out of hand, that they no longer enjoyed the cultural
or political authority they once did, that somebody had
better do something before it was too late. Some at least saw

their salvation in the examples of good art that filled the Crystal Palace.

This confidence in the soothing effects of exposure to art got a test of sorts one day when the ladies of the Five Points Mission School brought 100 of their students up to the Crystal Palace on a field trip. Restless and wild, the children hailed from "one of the most morally degraded spots on this wide earth." The good ladies expected them to be transformed in the Crystal Palace, their "unsophisticated tastes" given new force and direction by the many beautiful objects displayed there. But things didn't go according to plan. Though well behaved, the children showed more interest in toys and ice cream than art. "Our *young ladies* only wished for the handsome dresses and big dolls! Machinery, painting and statuary failed to awaken their admiration, and as this evidence of genuine taste was not particularly flattering," reported the rather nonplussed missionaries. They vowed to try "our philosophy" again at a more "favorable opportunity" but neglected to reveal whether that would require another field trip to the Crystal Palace.[17]

Thousands of our younger mechanics, artisan and laborers were intended "to regard the mighty Exhibition, not as a vast curiosity shop or raree-show," Greeley wrote in the preface to *Art and Industry*, "but as the grandest and most instructive University ever opened to themselves or their children on this continent." Like those children of the Five Points, however, they had their own ideas and seemed curiously unwilling to be schooled. City residents, working people especially, didn't visit the Crystal Palace as often as expected, or in the numbers predicted, reported the *Tribune*, "while country people and those from other towns than New-York flock to it." Besides, a majority of these sightseeing tourists from out of town, said the *Times*, will spend only a few hours, a day or two at most, "wandering about the building and inspecting the collection which it contains,—pausing here and there before those works of genius and skill which stand out at every turn, but carrying away only a confused recollection of silks, statuary, machinery, jewelry, minerals, and pictures." A wilderness of objects indeed.[18]

-·◦●◦●◦·-

One day in mid-August, 1853, workmen hauled a large crate into the Crystal Palace and set it on a pedestal near the much-maligned figure of Daniel Webster. When a rumor went around that the mysterious crate contained the statue of a naked woman called *The Greek Slave* (1844)—the work of expatriate sculptor Hiram Powers—a crowd began to gather, drawn by the prospect of glimpsing something usually "forbidden or unseen" (Figure 3.13). *The Greek Slave* was arguably

the most widely known work of its kind on either side if the Atlantic. Slightly different versions of it had been on tour for almost a decade. In Europe, it won high marks at the 1851 London Exhibition, while in America, where it was the first representation of a female nude to meet with public favor, many thousands of people in a dozen cities had lined up for a chance to see it for themselves. As it happened, however, the crate held *Eve Tempted* (1842), an earlier nude by Powers never before seen in the United States and only recently recovered from the same shipwreck that killed the writer and feminist Margaret Fuller on her way home from Italy with her husband and son. *The Greek Slave* was in a different box, waiting to be opened another day.[19]

Previously, Americans had always decried female nudity in works of art as scandalously salacious. But both *Eve* and *The Greek Slave* aroused little of this prudish hostility because

LEFT [FIGURE 3.13] The Greek Slave by the celebrated American sculptor Hiram Powers, 1846. Said the *Illustrated Magazine of Art:* "The Eve of Powers, if we except his own Greek Slave, comes nearer the requirements of art than any other work in the Exhibition" (2 (1853), 263). After he finished the original marble version of *The Greek Slave* in Florence in 1844, Powers made five full-size replicas for private collectors. Two toured the United States between 1847 and 1851; one was shown to great acclaim at the Crystal Palace in 1851. In an accompanying pamphlet Powers drew attention to the things that made the young woman's nudity acceptable: her touching attempt at modesty, her air of Christian resignation, the cross beneath her right hand, and a perdurable Western tradition about the sexual free-for-all awaiting her in the harem. Courtesy of The National Gallery of Art.)

Powers shielded each sculpture with an appealing moral narrative—the biblical account of the Fall in the first case and, in the second, the story of a proud young—and white—Christian woman abducted and sold into slavery by lascivious Turks during the Greek struggle for independence. For *The Greek Slave* in particular this narrative authorized crowds to look upon the woman's nakedness as an essential ingredient of her tragic though certain fate in some sultan's harem. As Powers himself said, her spirit, not her person, stood exposed to the lustful gaze of her captors. She wasn't really naked at all but clothed in virtue.[20]

How many people took this convenient tale seriously is impossible to tell, though it irritated abolitionists, who scolded Powers for ignoring slavery closer to home, and it squared with widespread assumptions about depraved, heathenish Ottomans. Nor was it immediately clear what statues of naked women were doing among all those steam engines, much less how they could help the march of industry. It seems unlikely, however, that anyone would have failed to pick up some rather disturbing erotic messages from *The Greek Slave*—messages of sexual conquest, bondage, subjugation, and degradation.

RIGHT [FIGURE 3.14 a, b, c, d, and e] Examples of the nudes or semi-nudes that were ubiquitous in the New York Crystal Palace. (*The World of Science, Art, and Industry, Illustrated from Examples in the New-York Exhibition, 1853–54*. Images a–d courtesy of Columbia University Libraries; image e courtesy of Museum of the City of New York.)

Often overlooked, at any rate, is the reality that the Crystal Palace had many more nudes on display than just *Eve* and the *Greek Slave*. Statues of naked or half-naked men, women, and children, but mostly women, greeted visitors throughout the building—"Venuses, Dianas, Joves, Cupids, Psyches and Apollos are strewn every where with true Italian profusion," *Putnam's* reported, accompanied by "hosts of pretty little, naughty Cupids, singly and in pairs, asleep and wide awake, in nests and in cages, and doing all sorts of mischief." (Figures 3.14 and 3.15) Remarkably, however, no one seems to have complained, although Horace Greeley, sounding a bit prissy, dismissed the entirety of American sculpture as "infantile" and contended that the people of the republic needed a more "severely correct taste" where that branch of art was concerned.[21]

Meanwhile, the Crystal Palace Association held its long-a-waited annual meeting at the Metropolitan Hotel in the closing days of February 1854. Things were every bit as bad as they feared, stockholders learned. Although it reported ticket sales thus far of almost $350,000—at $0.25 a head the equivalent of roughly 1.2 million visitors to the Crystal Palace—the Association still owed creditors $125,000. It had even

RIGHT [FIGURE 3.15] This cage of cupids from Italy "explains itself," said Silliman and Goodrich coyly (*Science, Art, and Industry, 50*). (Image: *Science and Mechanism: Illustrated by Examples in the New York Exhibition, 1853–4*. Courtesy of University of California Libraries.)

mortgaged the building to make ends meet, a setback the board blamed on the fact that construction had fallen so far behind schedule.[22]

The stockholders were out for blood and, as the *Times* explained with studied delicacy, "very naturally desire to place the concern in the hands of men, who have had more experience in catering for the public curiosity than the gentleman by whom it has thus far been managed." After several days of rancorous debate—highlighted by the appearance of no fewer than three separate slates of candidates—twenty-five men were finally elected to a new Board of Directors. Six of the twenty-five were holdovers from the old Board (Livingston, Foster, Nicholson, Whetten, Sherman, and Sedgwick). The nineteen new faces included Mayor Jacob Westervelt (renowned shipbuilder), Thomas B. Stillman (a founding partner of the Novelty Iron Works), Dudley Persse (a paper dealer and manufacturer), William O'Brien (broker), Edward Haight (banker), John T. Parrish (merchant), William B. Dinsmore (Adams Express Co.), John H. Cornell (banker), Henry Hilton (lawyer), John H. White (lawyer), James B. Brewster (coachmaker), George B. Butler (editor, *Journal of Commerce*), Warren Leland (owner and operator of the Metropolitan Hotel), Erastus C. Benedict (lawyer), Charles H. Haswell (civil engineer), William M. Chauncey (merchant), Charles Butler (merchant), and Horace Greeley of the *Tribune*. Easily the most controversial of the lot was Greeley's friend, proprietor of the American Museum on Broadway, Phineas Taylor Barnum (Figure 3.16).[23]

To describe P. T. Barnum as one of the more conspicuous characters in the city would be an understatement. At six feet two inches, with electric blue eyes, a head of curly brown hair, and an unexpectedly squeaky voice, he stood out in any crowd. More to the point, since arriving in New York from Connecticut twenty years earlier, Barnum had earned a reputation for such popular hoaxes and novelties as Joice Heth (a blind slave woman he said was George Washington's wet nurse), the Feejee Mermaid (really a mummified monkey), General Tom Thumb (a two-foot-tall dwarf), and flea circuses, among other things, many of which would be on view at his museum. He didn't lack for money, either. It was said that he earned a princely $500,000 just sponsoring Jenny Lind's concert tour of America in 1850. Two years later he branched out into publishing with a weekly New York paper, the *Illustrated News*, which devoted (until it folded) a gratifying number of pages to events on Reservoir Square. If P. T. Barnum couldn't make the Crystal Palace pay, nobody could.[24]

Not every stockholder welcomed Barnum's election to the board, to be sure. One called the Crystal Palace the "crowning glory of New York" and said the public expected it to remain "an arena for artistic competition, and not a mere toy shop for

[FIGURE 3.16] P. T. Barnum, portrait dated between 1855 and 1865. (Courtesy of the Library of Congress)

common huckstering." Everybody knew what he was talking about.[25]

Barnum, too, had his doubts. He recalled in his autobiography that Edward Riddell had asked him back in 1851 to help bring a Crystal Palace to New York, but he refused because he thought it followed too closely on the heels of its London prototype and would only lose money. Time proved him right. Still, the building had done some good. "Many thousands of strangers were brought to New-York, and however disastrous the enterprise may have proved to the stockholders, it is evident that the general prosperity of the city has been promoted far beyond the entire cost of the whole speculation." So, in 1854, when "numerous influential gentlemen" persuaded him to put his name forward for election to the new Board of the Crystal Palace Association, he agreed, "much against my own judgment." A week later the Board asked him to replace Sedgwick as president of the Association. Again, he said yes—providing he could see the books and verify that any semblance of "vitality" remained in the organization. If not, he reserved the right to quit.[26]

For the next several months, Barnum struggled to resuscitate the Association. He personally loaned it "large sums of money" to pay its creditors, in return for which he received a mortgage on the Crystal Palace worth $40,000. He successfully raised additional funds by convincing the city's businessmen, hotel owners, and railroad operators to purchase thousands of tickets in advance. He closed the building for a month to make "alterations" and promised a spectacular "re-inauguration" for the beginning of May (Figure 3.17). He recruited new exhibitors, pledged to group exhibits by type rather than by country of origin "to facilitate inspection," and agreed to let exhibitors have space free of charge while also allowing them advertise the prices of items they wished to sell. He negotiated with steamboat and rail companies for reduced fares between New York and the fashionable resorts of Newport or Cape May, slashed the price of admission to the Crystal Palace, and promised reasonable prices in its refreshment saloons. "I never labored so hard, night and day," he said later.[27]

On the whole, things went more smoothly for Barnum than they had for Sedgwick. Orson Munn, owner-publisher of *Scientific American*, frustrated Barnum's fundraising efforts when he sued the Association, alleging the old Board had borrowed upwards of $400,000 in violation of its charter. The suit was dropped in mid-April, after Barnum promised to buy a couple of hundred shares of Crystal Palace stock from Munn and his partners at $71 per share within six months. The deal didn't come soon enough, however, to prevent Munn from getting an injunction that made it impossible for the new Board to settle accounts with all its creditors.[28]

LEFT [FIGURE 3.17] Sculpture encircling the fountain after Barnum's 1854 renovation, which reportedly brought the number of "marbles" to almost 200. The unfortunate statue of Washington was moved to one side. (New-York Daily Times, April 17, 1854.)

The beginning of Barnum's presidency also coincided with the publication of an uncomplimentary report by a British commission sent the year before to inspect the New York Exhibition. The six-man commission was chaired by the Earl of Ellesmere, noted patron of the arts, and included Sir Charles Lyell, the foremost geologist of his day; Joseph Whitworth, a wealthy manufacturer and civil engineer; and George Wallis, the prominent art educator and designer. The commission arrived in June 1853 and attended the opening-day festivities at the Crystal Palace. But, as Lord Ellesmere explained, when they realized that the Exhibition would not in fact be finished for months yet, they split up and toured the country instead, visiting numerous cities and inspecting natural resources. Necessarily, therefore, their final verdict on the Exhibition was mixed. On the one hand, they found that the aspirations of the Crystal Palace Association had plainly exceeded their abilities. On the other, the commissioners met with "courtesy, attention and anxiety to assist" everywhere they went, and the Exhibition "may be said to be successful" in so far as "industrious artisans and enterprising manufacturers" will learn from it "what has to be done."[29]

It isn't clear whether the commissioners were bending over backwards to find something good to say about Exhibition, or just damning it with faint praise. Either way, they didn't slow down Barnum. He pressed on with his plans for the "re-inau-guration" of the Crystal Palace, now set for May 4.

And Barnum knew how to keep everyone on schedule. After a night of heavy rain, that event, dubbed a "popular Coronation of Labor" by the showman himself, began at 11:00 a.m. sharp with a parade that formed in front of City Hall. Barnum, waving his umbrella like a conductor's baton, herded everybody into place—a band of music in the lead, followed by veterans, officers of the Association, the clergy, various civic officials, delegates from each of the municipal trades, the police, and representatives of the army and navy. After circling City Hall Park, the procession swung uptown via Broadway and Sixth Avenue, arriving just after 12:30 at Reservoir Square, where a crowd of some 10,000—"composed in great part of ladies," according to the *Tribune*—had gathered outside the Crystal Palace. When it began to drizzle again, lucky ticketholders hurried inside for a performance of the "Hallelujah Chorus," a prayer, and a long afternoon of speechifying. "All of the front of the galleries, all the great stairways and portions of the lower floor, were crowded with bright faces of beauty and intelligence shining amid the gay colors of the present fashion of ladies' dresses." A second round of speeches followed that evening.

Compared to the year before, the 1854 re-inauguration was by most accounts something of a disappointment. The procession proved smaller than anticipated. The crowds along Broadway and Sixth Avenue, while enthusiastic, were noticeably thinner. This time, too, no politicians or generals competed for attention on the platform. In their place was a smaller number of men sympathetic to working people: Horace Greeley, Parke Godwin, the Rev. Henry Ward Beecher, Elihu Burritt, the Rev. E. H. Chapin, and a smattering of labor leaders, among others. They said little or nothing that had not been said before—that the Exhibition would inspire peaceful competition between nations, that labor alone creates value, that luxury should not be rejected out of hand, and so forth, while Greeley assured the audience that the Crystal Palace will show workers a nobler, happier, more cerebral way of life:

> To-day the apprentice or workman in our City looks forward to the end of his day's work as the beginning of its enjoyment. He throws down the implements of his labor of the moment the clock strikes six, and makes haste to prepare for and indulge in the evening's recreations. And, in order that these may *be* recreations, it is essential that they remind him of anything else rather than his work. The raree-show, the theatre, the negro melodists—too often the grogshop, and perhaps the gambling-house also—secure his nightly attention; while hardly one in a hundred devotes the evening habitually to

such observations or studies as would fit him to discharge more admirably the duties of the day.

In any event, this lack of originality hardly mattered. As usual, only a few members of the audience could hear the speakers, thanks to the lamentable acoustics of the cavernous building and thanks as well to the commotion caused when those who, unable catch a word, walked away en masse.[30]

Soon enough, Barnum realized that all his efforts to infuse new life into the Exhibition got him exactly nowhere. When he started a program of Sunday concerts he was scolded for trying "to introduce the French and German disregard of the Sabbath into an American city." His grand Musical Congress, featuring 1,500 performers, was lampooned in the press as "a humbug" because half the audience couldn't hear a note. He engaged John Wise, the famous American balloonist, to make an ascension from the grounds of Crystal Palace, but the event ended badly when Wise crashed near Flushing and tumbled out of the basket—whereupon the balloon sailed off again, finally coming to ground near a village in northeastern Connecticut.[31]

Arguably the one bright spot that dismal summer—at least in retrospect—was the demonstration by Elisha Otis of a safety mechanism he had invented for freight elevators. Devices for moving goods (and people) between the floors of multistory buildings had been around for years, of course. James Bogardus incorporated one into his design for the Crystal Palace, and Latting's Observatory was supposed to have had a steam elevator, though he never actually installed it. What Otis contributed was an automatic emergency brake that stopped a platform or car from falling if the lifting cable broke. At the Crystal Palace, he attracted a lot of attention because his "elevator"—a platform riding between four vertical rails— was too tall to be set up anywhere but under the dome, where it was visible to everyone, and especially because of the "apparent daring" of the inventor himself, who, according to the *Tribune*, "as he rides up and down upon the platform, occasionally cuts the rope by which it is supported." How often Otis pulled this Barnumesque stunt is unreported. Certainly no one at the time could foresee the revolutionary implications of his invention for the design and use of high-rise buildings.[32]

Certainly, too, there's no reason to believe that Otis's audacity improved attendance—which was bad news for Barnum, who finally resigned his post in early July 1854. Try as he might, said an Ohio paper, the great showman could not save the Crystal Palace. "His usual amount of humbuggery, mammoth concerts, Sunday performances, and other tricks of the trade, were not enough to save the concern." Barnum, for his part, couldn't conceal his disgust. "I was an

ass for having anything to do with the Crystal Palace," he confided to a friend.

·ー◦◦◉◦◦·

To succeed Barnum, the Association chose John H. White, a
local attorney and trustee. It also decided to close the Exhibition
for good at the end of October and auction off any unclaimed
contents. Predictably, the price of Association stock plum-
meted overnight. Exhibitors vanished, visitors disappeared,
and, in the words of the *Times*, Reservoir Square became "deserted and barren" again. "Only a few grogshops remain to tell
of the enterprises which were once flourishing and green in
those parts."[33]

By the autumn of 1854, the Crystal Palace had been reduced
to what *Harper's* once dismissed as a "glittering mausoleum of
happy hopes and betrayed confidences." There was some talk
about tearing the building down and selling it for scrap or
reassembling it elsewhere—in, say, Philadelphia, or maybe
Boston—though nothing came of either idea. When the time
came to auction off the remaining contents of the Crystal
Palace, the event had to be canceled for lack of interest. But
the last word came from a newspaper in the relatively new
town of Columbus, Ohio. The *Ohio State Journal* regretted
that the entire experience had been such a disaster for investors.

"In spite of all the sneers upon it, the Exhibition has been most important to the country," the paper editorialized. "It will be a long time before we shall again see such a magnificent and beautiful edifice as the Palace, or such a collection of statuary and paintings as have been on exhibition there."[34]

FOUR

The Widowed Bride of Sixth Avenue

"WHAT SHALL BE done with the Crystal Palace?" wondered the *Times* in the spring of 1855. "It is the most beautiful building in New York," echoed *Putnam's*. "But what will you do with it?" Everyone in town seemed to have had the same question, now that the Exhibition of the Industry of All Nations was over and chastened investors weighed options for cutting their losses. Quite a few of the sideshows in the neighborhood of Reservoir Square had moved elsewhere in search of greener pastures, leaving "the queen of buildings" standing, forlorn, "like a widowed bride on the Sixth-avenue." The Latting Observatory, too, had gone out of business, sold to a marble company that for unknown reasons sliced seventy-five feet off the top.

Inside the Crystal Palace, many exhibitors had long since cleared out, and in place of the numerous "policemen, doormen, ticket-sellers, money-counters and money-spenders," according to the *Tribune*, sat a solitary cashier who, for twenty-five cents, would let curiosity-seekers wander the musty, almost empty aisles. Moreover, the Crystal Palace Association had been dissolved and its assets entrusted to a receiver who should either remove the building from Reservoir Square or give it to the city, as the lease seemed to require. The Common Council of New York was bombarded with appeals to tear down the Crystal Palace or—inasmuch as it was still "the City's central attraction" and too important to its emerging network of hotels and restaurants—use it instead for a "nice respectable" produce market, a rail terminal, or perhaps a museum for the exhibition of "minerals, plants, animals, and other natural curiosities."

At the same time, the great economic boom of the early 1850s slowed markedly over the winter of 1854–55. Every day brought news of more bankruptcies, more layoffs, more evictions, more hunger—and louder demands from labor leaders that the city take immediate steps to freeze rents, expand the system of outdoor relief, or guarantee employment for everyone. But the economy roared to life again with the return of warm weather, and these measures, so out of keeping with the liberal, laissez-faire assumptions of upper-class New Yorkers—

and those who aspired to the upper classes—soon lost momentum.[1]

-·◦◉◦·-

Against this background, *Scientific American*'s Orson Munn dragged Barnum into court, accusing the ex-president of re-neging on his promise of the year before to purchase the shares of Crystal Palace stock owned by Munn and his partners. A jury awarded them $15,235—but not before local papers recapped all the follies and failures of the Association. Of course, none of this legal wrangling resolved the question of what the building could possibly be used *for*.[2]

One prospect emerged at the end of June 1855, when the first pieces of the famous "Washingtonea Gigantea or Monster Tree of California!" arrived at the Crystal Palace. Thirty-one feet in diameter and over 300 feet high, this "mastodon" Sequoia was—allegedly—older than the Pyramids and a contemporary of Moses and the Prophets. When offi-cially unveiled on the Fourth of July, it drew an estimated 7,000 visitors, who paid twenty-five cents apiece to see it. But predictions of bigger crowds to come proved overly optimis-tic after a skeptical reporter pointed out that the pieces of the sliced-up tree appeared to have been reassembled incor-rectly, possibly from more than one specimen, proclaiming it

"a gigantic sell," comparable to wooly horses, mermaids, and similar wonders popular among the most credulous elements of the population. Subsequently set up in London's Crystal Palace (newly relocated to Sydenham Hill in 1854), the "vegetable curiosity" appears to have had a friendlier reception (Figure 4.1).[3]

What about renting out the Crystal Palace for special events—balls, rallies, conventions, lectures, and the like? This possibility came in for a lot of discussion in the autumn of 1855, when the new Association of Publishers hired the building for a great Literary Banquet that saw 400 of its members, booksellers included, break bread with 200 authors. But New York had as yet to be recognized as the premier American venue for such gatherings, besides which the demand for big, spectacular places to convene was probably still quite limited. It wasn't even clear that the Association of Publishers would survive.[4]

Similar events would follow over the next several years: a convention of inventors, a meeting to plan "a Great Sabbath-School Celebration," a "grand Promenade Concert" of the African American Odd Fellows, a wedding or two, and so on.[5]

Most promising was the decision of the American Institute to move its Annual Fair into the Crystal Palace. Ever since its

LEFT [FIGURE 4.1] The giant California sequoia on display in the Crystal Palace, Sydenham. (English Heritage)

founding thirty years earlier, the American Institute—officially the American Institute for the Encouragement of Science and Invention—had been one of the country's most respected advocates for mechanization and industrial progress. Over the years, the Institute's annual shows (most recently held on the Battery in Castle Garden, known today as Castle Clinton), proved extremely popular and won acclaim for showcasing early examples of American ingenuity, including Colt's revolver, Morse's telegraph, Singer's sewing machine, and McCormick's reaper. The meetings of its principal divisions such as the Farmer's Club never failed to draw appreciative, if modest, audiences for learned presentations on topics like manure management, grafting wax, noxious weeds in Russian agriculture, or the new Gibbs Rotary Digging Machine. In 1853, however, the Institute lost "thousands of dollars" and nearly succumbed to stiff competition from the Exhibition in the Crystal Palace, which had a very similar message but a more interesting building. In 1854, its managers canceled the fair altogether. In 1855, they announced that they would try again, this time in the Crystal Palace itself, as soon as the authors and publishers got out of the way.[6]

When the fair opened, visitors found a wider selection of "art and industry" than had been on display at the Exhibition in 1853. Not only did the managers of the event claim to have "more articles of invention and utility" that testified to American progress, but they had inherited many of the Exhibition's most popular paintings and statuary as well— among them Thorvaldsen's group, *Christ and the Apostles,* still a crowd-pleaser. Both of the two refreshment saloons remained open, the north nave remained set up for heavy machinery, and the giant California sequoia remained standing under the dome. Yet there was also plenty that people hadn't seen before—a magnificent display of fruits and flowers, for example, a steam-driven machine for splitting firewood, Bramble's automatic grain scale, an elevated railroad that continuously circled inside the building, directly "over the head of visitors," a clever device for washing windows, an even cleverer "petticoat lifter" that used hidden pulleys to enable a lady to go up and down stairs in a hooped skirt "with perfect grace." The Institute also sponsored contests that attracted enthusiastic throngs. A high point by all reports was the competition between fire engines, won by a pumper from Brooklyn which shot a stream of water 162 feet up the side of the former, and now somewhat truncated, Latting Observatory.[7]

* * *

Attendance at the Institute's fair ran higher than expected during the roughly six weeks it stayed open—indeed, the managers said they'd actually turned a profit—in light of which there were calls for it to occupy the Crystal Palace permanently. The Institute tried to buy the building and all its contents but couldn't agree with the court-appointed receiver, John H. White, on a price. For the next several years they nevertheless continued to rent the Crystal Palace for their annual fall fair, which usually got under way in mid-September or early October. They also became a prominent advocate for municipal ownership of the building on the theory that the city would always rent it to them at a favorable rate.[8]

Around the beginning of 1856, if not sooner—partly because he hoped the Crystal Palace might yet repay the cost of construction, partly because he appreciated its economic importance to the city, and partly because he didn't have the money to take it down anyway—receiver White decided to seek an extension of the five-year lease on Reservoir Square, due to expire the following January. His apparently innocuous request sparked no end of trouble with people who, like the managers of the American Institute, had their own ideas about what should be done with the Crystal Palace.

At times, the ensuing controversy nearly got out of hand. When White petitioned the City Council to extend the lease, for example, local property owners, claiming the city had promised to turn Reservoir Square into a public park and that White was supposed to deliver it in its original condition, cried foul. The Council's Committee on Lands and Places went on record opposing the petition. White then said he would take his case to the state legislature, dominated by Republicans, a move not calculated to find favor with the Democratic administration of Mayor Fernando Wood. Meanwhile, in May 1856 the Committee on Lands and Places invited White to appear and give reasons for extending the lease. White's colloquy with a certain James P. Banks, who owned multiple lots facing Reservoir Square, went off the rails as soon as White proposed that the committee go up to inspect the neighborhood for itself:

MR. WHITE—We will all go in the same carriage.

MR. BANKS—No; we won't, Sir. You won't go in any carriage I go in, if I am the stronger, I know.

MR. WHITE—I should like to see the whole affair [i.e., the Crystal Palace] remain.

MR. BANKS—Yes, but it has got to come down. [Laughter.]

MR. WHITE—I have heard such threats before.

MR. BANKS—You never saw me before.

MR. WHITE—You have made them.

MR. BANKS—You never saw me before in your life.

MR. WHITE—And if our acquaintance is not carried on with more amenity, it will be very desirable that we never should see each other again.

MR. BANKS—I hope we shan't meet any more...

MR. WHITE—If my suggestion is accepted, and I cannot prove it to be proper to hold on to this Palace, then I shall be content with anything that the Committee may decide upon.

MR. BANKS—You will have to be. (To the Committee.) His facts ain't facts, for they only exist in his imagination. The Crystal Palace was only got up to make money of. You will hardly see an individual in the neighborhood who does not consider it a complete nuisance. It is open all day and all night, Sunday and all, and the tenements around there—

MR. WHITE—Are any owned by you? [Laugh.]

MR. BANKS—Hold your tongue, Sir—[Exhibitions?] described by this big MR. WHITE, this magnanimous MR. WHITE, this great MR. WHITE, this renowned MR. WHITE, are a great nuisance, and until that Palace, as they please to term it, is brought down it will be one. There are all sorts of disgraceful scenes carried on there—there are rum holes, beef holes, &c., &c. [Indignation evident in the speaker, and laughter general.]

The gentleman says it is a great ornament, and he says that that is well known. It is no ornament, and he can't make it one. It is a receptacle for the commission of sins and nuisances, a blackguard concern altogether.

MR. WHITE—The very reason the [Committee] should go up and see it.

MR. BANKS—Mr. Curly-head, will you stop? [Laughter.] ... Will someone stop that man? or I will. [Laughter.]

MR. WHITE—It was understood it [i.e., Reservoir Square] was for a public use.

MR. BANKS—Go away; I don't want you to talk. (To the Committee)—D—n him, I don't like to see him at all. Excuse me, gentlemen of the Committee, but I don't like to hear a man speak that I do not believe to be decently honest. (To MR. WHITE)—I would insult you, but I believe you are too great a coward to take an insult.

MR. WHITE—You are too old a man; it would be beneath me to take an insult from you.

Mr. Banks—I am young yet. I would whip you in two minutes. (To the Committee.)—This shameful place is open night and day.

Mr. White—That is not true. . . . You know better.

Mr. Banks—What is that you little scoundrel. Do you say that I tell a lie. You are the greatest liar, the greatest scoundrel, the greatest coward [not clear] and out of the State Prison.[9]

The Committee on Lands and Places adjourned—reluctantly, one imagines—calling a halt to this merry exchange before the two men came to blows. White still could not get the lease renewed, however, and decided over the summer that the city ought to buy the Crystal Palace from him instead.

······

Late one night at the end of August, fire broke out in an old building on the northeast corner of Sixth Avenue and 43rd Street shared by a cooper's shop and a storeroom for the Sixth Avenue Railroad Company. The conflagration spread quickly, consuming two dozen or more tenements and leaving a large number of poor families homeless. It then leapt across 43rd to the wooden Latting Observatory, which burned like a torch—"a monument of flame reaching to the clouds amid the darkness and smoke!" wrote the *Times* rapturously (Figure 4.2). "It looked like a pyrotechnic display on a Fourth of July evening," enthused the *Brooklyn Eagle*, which "the dome of the Crystal Palace opposite, and the glass surface of the building generally, reflected brilliantly." Several times firemen feared the observatory would topple over onto the Crystal Palace, but that building escaped serious harm, though six bushels of red-hot embers were swept off its roof and heat of the inferno raging just across the street melted the solder between some of the glass panels. The wind came up and reportedly blew cinders from the fire—now ranked as one of the grandest anyone had seen in years—as far away as St. Mark's Place, two miles downtown, while a resident of Carmel, fifty-five miles to the north in Putnam County, claims to have watched "flames shoot up into the sky," though he didn't learn until later what had burned. Reports of a man seen coming out of the cooper's shop just before the fire was discovered fueled the inevitable rumors of arson. One way or the other, despaired the *Herald*, visitors to New York will be unable to "take in at one glance this great metropolis, but must be content to view it in sections."[10]

Repairing the damage to the Crystal Palace, as well as the loss of the old Latting Observatory, slowed White only momentarily. By early 1857, when the lease finally ran out and the use of Reservoir Square automatically reverted to the City of New York, he had resumed his efforts to sell the Crystal Palace to the municipality. "It was the only building of the kind on this continent," he reminded the Committee on Lands and Places, "and the commercial metropolis should own it." It was a bargain, too. Although it cost over $700,000 to build, and was worth $80,000 as scrap, he would part with the structure for only $150,000 (Barnum had figured anything under $300,000 would be "dog cheap"). But as Mayor Wood explained about the same time, the question to be decided was whether the city didn't *already* own it by virtue of the expiration of the lease on Reservoir Square.[11]

The managers of American Institute, for their part, resolved there was no two ways about it: the city no longer had to buy the Crystal Palace because *it was now municipal property*. So one wintry day in January 1857 they got themselves appointed as

DESTRUCTION OF THE LATTING OBSERVATORY, NEW YORK.

unpaid custodians of the building and its remaining contents and boldly marched up Broadway to seize it in the name of the municipality. Victory speeches ensued, accompanied by (this according to the *Tribune*) a great deal of tobacco spitting. Things got a bit tense when one of the exhibitors tried to remove some personal effects, only to be told that everything now belonged to the American Institute. A crisis was averted when none other than receiver White, still hoping to sell the Crystal Palace to the city, showed up at the last minute and unceremoniously threw out the managers. Thus ended their little "fillibustering expedition" (the *Tribune*'s words again), though who owned the Crystal Palace was still a matter of opinion.

Thus caught in legal and political limbo, the Crystal Palace slowly deteriorated, inasmuch as none of the contending parties would take full responsibility for maintenance. (Proper maintenance cost money: it would require employing forty full-time glaziers, the council learned, "just to keep the glass in.") That March *Putnam's* called the Crystal Palace "a melancholy sight now." At the end of May, a special committee of the City Council heard testimony that the several thousand

LEFT [FIGURE 4.2] The burning of the Latting Observatory. "A sheet of flame perfectly white," wrote *The Pittsfield Sun* on Sept. 4, 1856, "extended from the bottom to the top of the building...a fearful but brilliant sight to the thousands on the ground. The whole northern part of the city was illuminated." Note the dome of the Crystal Palace across the street. (Courtesy of the Museum of the City of New York)

screws and "perhaps millions of bolts" holding it together were so badly rusted an entire year might be needed to dismantle it. Toward the close of August 1857, as the American Institute prepped for its annual fair (and, as we will see, the city grappled with a spreading financial panic) the *Times* sent a reporter to check on rumors that the Crystal Palace was "a miserable wreck, open on all sides to the action of wind and rain." While those rumors were exaggerated, the paper said, one of the skylights was indeed "somewhat defective," which it knew because during a recent storm the floor beneath it got soaked. In March of the following year, the *Times* took White's side and urged the city to buy the Crystal Palace, "this sadly-neglected pleasure-house of the people," before it fell apart. One Sunday night in the summer of 1858, a chandelier suspended beneath the great dome broke away from its moorings and came down with a "tremendous crash." No one was hurt, but the warning was unmistakable.[12]

Complicating the question of what to do with the Crystal Palace was the continuing deterioration of social relations in the city, which the Exhibition—contrary to the intentions and expectation of some—had done nothing to improve. An alarming uptick in street violence in the building's final two or three years gave genteel New Yorkers new reasons to fear that law and order in the city would collapse and leave them at the mercy of the mob.

In June 1854, one J. S. Orr, an itinerant preacher known as the "Angel Gabriel," came down from New England, where he probably became affiliated in one capacity or other with the xenophobic Know-Nothing movement. His loony rants against Catholicism had triggered bloody rioting in Boston, and his debut in Brooklyn likewise touched off a riot in which the police reportedly emptied their revolvers into the crowd. Orr then crossed the river to Manhattan, trailed by predictions of worse trouble in New York. Aside from a bit of fighting in City Hall Park, nothing untoward happened, perhaps because the police showed up with clubs. Later that same year, Gabriel again preached to the multitude from the steps of City Hall, accompanied by Moses and "St. Paul." This time, it took the militia and 500 police to keep the peace—though the propertied classes, a mostly Protestant elite in a city with a large Irish Catholic population, had a good scare.[13]

Late in 1856, in a story about the barroom shooting of one African American by another, the *Times* speculated that "the colored fancy gentry" in New York had adopted "the example of the whites in carrying loaded pistols for manly defense in emergencies." Pistols weren't much help against the disorder that seemed to be engulfing the city. Although both 1855 and 1856 had been relatively quiet, the need for "manly defense" remained a matter of intense concern, particularly among those with something to defend. The city was again plunged into turmoil in April 1857, when the Republican legislature established a state-controlled Metropolitan police force on the not-implausible grounds that the current force had become too corrupt to combat crime.

Mayor Wood, a Democrat, gamely fought back, first in court and then by reorganizing the existing constabulary into a parallel organization, the Municipal police, personally loyal to him. For two months, while the Metropolitans and Municipals jockeyed for supremacy, the city's "riff-raff had a good time thieving, picking pockets, robbing houses," and murdering law-abiding citizens. It comes as no surprise, under the circumstances, that the mayor allowed the final dispensation of the Crystal Palace to drag on for so long.

On June 16, a party of Metropolitans showed up at Wood's office with a warrant for his arrest on the bogus charge of fomenting a riot. Waiting for them was a Praetorian Guard of Municipals. One thing led to another, push came to shove, and what the *Times* called "a terrible fight" erupted on the very steps of City Hall. "Many on both sides were felled to the ground, and blood spirted [sic] high from the wounds of the combatants," the paper reported; "blows upon naked heads fell thick and fast, and men rolled helplessly down the steps, to be leaped upon and beaten till life seemed extinct." The bloodshed didn't end until the militia waded in to rescue the

Metropolitans. Twenty-odd combatants were taken to area hospitals, several having what were thought to be mortal injuries. In early July, two weeks later, the New York Court of Appeals ruled against Wood, who abruptly dissolved the Municipals.[14]

Wood's capitulation simply prolonged the agony. On July 4, 1857, one day after the mayor gave in, the inexperienced Metropolitans failed to break up a fight between two rival gangs, the nativist Bowery Boys and the Irish Dead Rabbits. The conflict escalated rapidly. Barricades went up in Bayard and Mulberry streets, stones flew, and then guns came out. The battle raged for two days until general exhaustion, with the help of the militia, brought it to an end. At least six men died and a hundred lay wounded. A week later, the Metropolitans barely survived an attack by a predominantly German crowd.

New York had not seen anything like conflict on this scale at least since the Astor Place riot almost ten years earlier. To all intents and purposes, declared the *Times*, the city had become just another banana republic, distracted by "anarchy" and liable, like Nicaragua perhaps, to be conquered by the first dictator who comes along. By disbanding the Municipals before the Metropolitans were prepared to take over, Wood aided and abetted the "prowling ruffians" of the city, who are "as reckless as hungry wolves when they have any reason to believe that they will be permitted to indulge in their savage propensities." Yet in a remarkable essay on "Mobocracy," the paper also warned against draconian countermeasures, explaining that in the United States, as opposed to England or France, rioting and other such outrages need not mean imminent revolution because most people understand that they are a cost of freedom. Remember, too, the *Times* cautioned, the "wretched" instigators of the recent troubles in New York, "depraved scoundrels, as they evidently are," crave excitement as much as the next man. "The gratification which their wild, untrained natures find in strong drink and street-fights, richer and more fortunate men find in the theater, in hunting, in music, painting, reading and the society of friends, in travel and in the whirl of commerce and of the forum."

Rome wasn't built in a day, of course. "Moral and aesthetic tastes need training just as well as the physical palate, and you [cannot] expect a rowdy to turn at one jump from street-fights to the sober amusements of gentlemen and scholars." A few years earlier, recall, one argument for a Crystal Palace in New York was that it would tranquilize the rowdies by showing them the many and varied fruits of industrialization—by exhibiting the many commodities already on the market. Now, the *Times* at least appeared to have decided that the experiment was unsuccessful. Its preference was for stepped-up "missionary work" among the benighted inhabitants of slums like the Five Points, too poor to buy their way to gentility. Religion, not exhibitions, would be necessary to make them civilized.[15]

-••§••-

Clouding the future of the Crystal Palace still further was the Panic of 1857, an international crisis that began in August of that year when the Ohio Life Insurance and Trust—a supposedly rock-solid financial institution whose president, Charles Stetson, had served on the Board of the Crystal Palace Association—collapsed under pressure from creditors spooked by the company's risky loans and news that its manager had helped himself to company money. Hundreds of other firms around the country, caught in a tightening credit squeeze, were dragged down in the days and weeks that followed. By mid-October the banking system was buckling, business was at a standstill, half the brokers on Wall Street were unemployed, and the contagion was spreading across Europe and South America, proving that capitalism was now global in scope (welcome news for Marx, still ensconced in the British Library, who cheerfully confided to Engels, "Despite my financial distress, I have not felt so cozy since 1848."). By November, with winter coming on, tens of thousands of working men and women in New York alone were said to be looking for work.[16]

Mayor Wood came up with a plan to tap the unemployed for municipal projects like the new Central Park, paying them in cornmeal, potatoes, and flour. A few thousand at most ever got hired, while Wood himself was denounced for advocating "fiery communism" and class warfare, exciting "the laborer against the capitalist, the rich against the poor."

Affluent New Yorkers preferred rather more traditional forms of philanthropy, such as the fancy-dress charity balls hosted that winter at the new Academy of Music and elsewhere. The *ne plus ultra* of these events was the "colossal charity soiree" held at the Crystal Palace in early April 1858 under the auspices of the Hunter Woodis Benevolent Society. Newspapers promised "a grand affair"—"the most perfect, extensive and elegant of its kind"—"the most brilliant *fête*…which has ever delighted the world of New York"—"a greater gathering of celebrities than the 'oldest inhabitant' has ever yet witnessed," including four sitting governors, four mayors, and a visiting Turkish admiral, plus assorted military and naval officers. Inside, the managers installed hundreds of additional gas lights, prepared the floors for dancing, and set up a huge "supper room" that ran from 40th to 42nd Street. They also arranged with streetcar and stage companies to stay open longer than usual.[17]

On the appointed evening, a great crowd estimated at between 10,000 and 15,000 people elbowed into the Crystal Palace, gaping at the profusion of military gear (serenely unaware, it seems, that the ball's martial theme was a curious choice for an event supposed to help the hungry and homeless.) An awestruck *Times* reporter counted ninety army tents lining the naves, interspersed with "field-pieces, stands of arms, piles of drums, trophies of war, pikes, flags and javelins" on loan from the City Arsenal. By all accounts, the reporter wrote, everything was perfect, and the entire affair went off splendidly. Then he left to file his story before the deadline for the next morning's edition.

He left too early. Around 1:00 a.m., an "immense crowd" of people ready to go home rushed the cloakroom. A confused free-for-all ensued. Barricades were overturned, shelves knocked down, and—the bar having been "too freely patronized"—gentlemen began to pummel one another. In the widening pandemonium, women screamed, some wept "unrestrainedly," others fainted, and several hundred fled into the street, leaving behind heaps of coats, hats, wrappers, and (according to the *Herald*) "a great number of soiled hose, in advanced stages of decomposition." At 3:30, after more than two hours of this regrettable uproar, two men got into a knife fight, "diversifying the entertainment," though neither one suffered serious injuries. The only other casualty was one of the traumatized German women in charge of the cloakroom. She fainted dead away and "is likely to become a confirmed maniac from the effects of the excitement." Subsequently, as if this embarrassing fiasco wasn't enough, the Society had to answer charges that a great part of the money intended for poor relief had gone missing, perhaps siphoned off by the "knot of swindlers" who dreamed up the event in the first place.

Nothing further was heard from the Hunter Woodis Benevolent Society, which mysteriously vanished without explaining where the money went. For respectable, well-fed New Yorkers, memories of the Panic of 1857—and the terrible immiseration of so many of their fellow citizens—eventually faded, eclipsed by a sheen of renewed economic health and the Civil War.

In the meantime Wood's successor as mayor, the paint manufacturer Daniel F. Tiemann, seems to have made up his mind to get rid of the Crystal Palace once and for all. When a measure came before the legislature approving its purchase, Tiemann and the council pointed out that the city already owned the building (not to mention that it had run out of money) and would take it down if receiver White didn't do so by May 1858. At the end of that month, tired of waiting for him to quit stalling, the mayor and comptroller sent in the police, who took possession of the Crystal Palace and confiscated property allegedly worth $100,000 without opposition from anybody—other than White, persistent to the end, who showed up without warning, vowing to sue the person or persons behind this illegal coup d'état (his words), before they hustled him out the door.[18]

⋅∘∙◉∙∘⋅

If the City of New York really meant to dismantle the Crystal Palace, it was in no hurry to do so. The summer of 1858 came and went, and still the building remained standing on Reservoir Square, forlorn and slowly falling apart for lack of proper maintenance. On September 1, 1858, it was pressed into service as the northern terminus of a huge procession celebrating completion of the Atlantic Cable between England and America. "Cable-fever runs wild" in New York, wrote the *Times*, describing hotels overflowing with guests and sidewalks thronged with excited visitors from town. At 2:00 p.m. one of the largest, most enthusiastic crowds ever seen in the modern history of the city—over 15,000 strong by some accounts—began to leave the Battery and make its way up Broadway, past flag-draped buildings and dense masses of cheering spectators. At Madison Square, the procession swung into Fifth Avenue, then followed Fifth all the way up to Reservoir Square, which it reached at 6:30 p.m. (Figure 4.3). Those people with tickets then filed into the Crystal Palace for entertainments and speeches extolling the cable as well as the wondrous benefits it would bring. That evening's principal oration featured The Rev. David Dudley

[FIGURE 4.3] The great procession of September 1, 1858. If the sign advertising Mix's carriages is any indication, this photograph—from a stereocard—shows the marchers passing 440 Broadway, where Isaac Mix had his shop. (*Trow's New York City Directory for the Year Ending May 1, 1859* (New York, 1859), 565.) (Image courtesy of the New York Public Library)

Lith. of Sarony, Major & Knapp 449 Broadway N.Y.

THE ORATION AT CRYSTAL PALACE SEPT. 1ST 1858.

[FIGURE 4.4] The Crystal Palace, decorated for David D. Field's oration, looking east. Although provided tables near the platform, the press corps complained that— as usual—no one could hear the speakers. (Art & Picture Collection, The New York Public Library, Astor, Lenox and Tilden Foundations)

Field, who traced at great length the history of the efforts to lay the Atlantic cable and the crucial role of his brother, Cyrus West Field, a distinguished resident of New York and one of the "telegraphic heroes" (Figure 4.4). The festivities concluded with a spectacular late-night torchlight parade of 6,000 firemen back down Broadway, still jammed with onlookers, and a memorable display of fireworks in City Hall Park.[19]

No American city has ever witnessed a more "picturesque display," boasted the *Times*. It was "the greatest event of the age." Unfortunately, it also proved somewhat premature. On October 5, with the annual show of the American Institute just getting under way, and while everyone seemed to be focused on the Lincoln-Douglas debates out in Illinois, the Crystal Palace itself burned to the ground. Only weeks later the cable connecting the United States and England broke, not to be replaced for nearly a decade.

The Finest Building in America

In the days and weeks following the fire, news that the Crystal Palace was no more, spread by telegraph and railroad, cycled through magazines and newspapers around the country. Lithographers and engravers tried to convey the magnitude of the disaster with scenes of billowing smoke and raging flames and crowds of onlookers rushing back and forth (Figures 5.1 and 5.2). A medal was struck to commemorate the blaze (Figure 5.3), and John Kenan, a practitioner of the new art of photography

FOLLOWING PAGE [FIGURE 5.1] The Crystal Palace Fire, New York. This view is from the 42nd Street side of the building, looking south toward lower Manhattan. Sixth Avenue is on the right. The Croton Distributing Reservoir on Fifth Avenue is on the left. (Author's Collection)

[FIGURE 5.2] The Crystal Palace fire, by Currier & Ives—the view from Sixth Avenue. Just before the dome collapsed, the flames burned through the halyard attaching a large American flag to the cupola. Along with panels of tin from the roof, the flag floated off into the sunset. (Courtesy of the New York Public Library)

with a studio down on Maiden Lane, advertised a series of six stereoscopic views, since vanished, entitled "The Crystal Palace in Ruins."[1]

On the morning of October 6, 1858, disconsolate exhibitors began sifting through the smoldering rubble of the Crystal Palace for possessions that had survived the conflagration (Figure 5.4)—for the most part coming away empty-handed, though one man was observed by the *Herald* in the act of carrying off barrels of embers from the site of his display, "with a

THE CRYSTAL PALACE FOR THE EXHIBITION
OF THE INDUSTRY OF ALL NATIONS.
NEW YORK, 1853.

PRESIDENT: THEODORE SEDGWICK, ESQR:
ARCHITECTS:
MESSRS: CARSTENSEN & GILDEMEISTER,
LENGTH 365 FEET, WIDTH 365 FEET,
HEIGHT OF DOME 148 FEET,
GLAZED SURFACE 206,000 SUP FEET,
OCCUPIES 5 ACRES
OF GROUND.
ESTIMATED VALUE $450,000.

[FIGURE 5.3] Medal commemorating the destruction by fire of the Crystal Palace. (American Numismatic Society)

view to washing [them] for relics." Other scavengers merely wanted a souvenir of what the Reverend Edwin Hubbell Chapin called "one of the most beautiful buildings in the world." According to the *Times*, "the ruins are everywhere mixed up, and permeated with melted glass of every conceivable

[FIGURE 5.4] A view of the ruins of The Crystal Palace. "All else was a heap of ruin," said the Times two days after the fire, "an inextricably-confused mass of sheet-iron, charred wood, iron girders and rafters, wheels, beams, levers, axles, cogs, [and] coils." (Art & Picture Collection, The New York Public Library, Astor, Lenox and Tilden Foundations)

form. It is found sticking to everything…and is the article generally seized upon by those in search of mementos." Someone reportedly found a set of false teeth, intact but completely encased in the stuff.

For anyone unable or unwilling to dig through the debris by themselves, a certain Mrs. Richardson, identified in a handbill only as one of the burned-out exhibitors, offered to sell lumps of melted glass and iron retrieved from the site (Figure 5.5).

[FIGURE 5.5] A lump of glass salvaged from the ruins of the Crystal Palace. (Courtesy of Museum of the City of New York)

These "curiosities very valuable for a cabinet," as she described them, were all that remained of "the finest building ever erected in America" (Figure 5.6).

Overshadowed by the back and forth over whether or not an arsonist caused the 1858 fire is the more arresting question of whether the Crystal Palace was prudently or competently built to begin with. Early in 1853, drawing attention to repeated delays, *Scientific American* had reprinted an article from the *New-York Sun* alleging that "The engineers and architects are at loggerheads; much of the material has to be fitted after it reaches the ground, beams being found too long, and girders too short." Later that year, Carstensen himself complained of "gross blunders in patterns and measurements"

CRYSTAL PALACE
RELICS !

Mrs. RICHARDSON, of New York, (who was one of the unfortunate persons burnt out by the fire that destroyed the Crystal Palace,) by permission of the MAYOR OF NEW YORK, and of JOHN H. WHITE, Esq., Crystal Palace Receiver, obtained a number of curiosities very valuable for a cabinet, produced by the melting of the Building, and articles on exhibition, which she now offers to visitors at the FAIR AT PALACE GARDEN, as interesting souvenirs of all that remains of the finest building ever erected in America—a building made entirely of glass and iron, except the floors—and supposed to be almost wholly free from danger of fire; yet, it was utterly destroyed on the 5th of October, 1858, in fifteen minutes' time. The evidence of the immense heat will be seen in the articles now offered for sale, as well worthy the attention of the curious.

An interesting memorial of the great Crystal Palace Exhibition, is found in Mrs. RICHARDSON'S collection of Relics, which is on exhibition in the 2d floor. They consist of vitrified masses of glass, metals, &c., showing the intense heat which prevailed in the building at the time of its destruction.—THE SUN, Oct. 11.

Wynkoop, Hallenbeck & Thomas, Printers, 113 Fulton Street, N. Y.

during construction and explained that workmen routinely fell back on the "cutting and tying or scribe-rule process," i.e., the trial-and-error procedure more closely associated with, say, traditional carpentry than with precision metalwork. And in 1858, after the fire, the *American Phrenological Journal* remembered that New York's Crystal Palace had been built by "cut and try."

What this meant is that when columns or girders or other components of the building didn't square up according to specifications, workmen either had to make them fit with on-the-spot modifications or force them into proper alignment. In fact, said the *Phrenological Journal* "every part of [the Crystal Palace] had to be more or less sprung, in order to bring the parts into place." How a journal of phrenology came by this information remains unclear. Iron could be handled like lumber, though—up to a point. When the Crystal Palace opened, the exhibit by George Williston & Co. of Brunswick, Maine, included a "railroad iron straightener or curver; a heavy beam with clamps at the ends to hold the iron, which may be sprung to any shape by a screw and stirrup."

Imagine, then, the sequence of events as the flames spread along those varnished wooden floorboards of the Crystal

LEFT [FIGURE 5.6] Mrs. Richardson's handbill. It called the Crystal Palace "the finest building ever erected in America." (Courtesy of the Museum of the City of New York)

Palace. The several hundred cast-iron columns would begin to soften in the intense heat, lose structural integrity, and spring away from the wrought iron girders they were attached to—a possible reason for the odd sounds reported by some witnesses of the blaze. Unsupported, the galleries and their exhibits would then collapse onto the floor below, splintering joists and adding fuel to the fire. Only minutes would elapse before the iron panels and frames of the facade began to buckle and the growing conflagration consumed the wooden sashes that held the windows. A shower of broken, melting glass would then have fallen on anyone still in the building, though no one was, as we know. After the great dome itself fell with a loud crash shortly thereafter, the comparative silence must have seemed eerie.

If that is even close to the way it happened, one implication is that the adoption of new construction materials, at least in the United States, had rather obviously outpaced the adoption of appropriate construction methods and standards. It would certainly help explain why the Crystal Palace fell apart so fast in the 1858 fire.[2]

--∙∙◉◉◉∙∙--

Would the Crystal Palace be rebuilt or replaced, and by whom? There was surprisingly little interest in these issues after the fire. Indeed, the consensus seemed to be that it just wouldn't be worth the trouble—that New York didn't really *need* a Crystal Palace after all. There is a reason why its London prototype succeeded, according to the *Herald* (which never warmed to the Exhibition idea in the first place): people in that city had nowhere else to see what money could buy, no fine shops or fancy stores staffed with informed, accommodating clerks. New York—especially along Broadway—was another story altogether:

> Here we have in Broadway at least two miles of palaces. Within that magic area the efforts of the best artists and the cleverest mechanics may be found on view every day in the year, without money and without price. If a man paints a good picture, or invents a new flytrap, or has anything curious to show or to sell, he puts it in a Broadway bazaar for exhibition to a public that is always ready to look. If the ladies wish to see the latest importation from Europe...there are splendid palaces like Stewart's, while on every side rise edifices nearly as fine as his, and crowded with the choicest products of the world's industry.[3]

Broadway, the paper repeated, as if its point weren't already clear enough, "is the condensation of half a dozen Crystal Palaces in one great emporium of art, science, fashion, literature, and trade.... We can get along very well without Crystal Palace."

Mrs. Richardson's "curiosities" failed to anchor the Crystal Palace securely in popular memory, and all too soon the city forgot about it—for the reasons given by the *Herald*, not to mention the growing secessionist movement in the South. Constructing "the finest building in America" was nonetheless an important first step in the emergence of New York as a destination in its own right. Though the building lost money, it encouraged a new industrial bourgeoisie to see itself as the final arbiter of good taste and decorum. Its greatest achievement, however, may have been to show Americans that they, too, could put up a modern building every bit as beautiful— perhaps more beautiful—than the original.

NOTES

Prologue: The End

1. This account of the fire draws on the extensive coverage in the *New-York Daily Tribune*, Oct. 6, 7, and 8, 1858; the *New-York Daily Times*, Oct. 6, 7, 11, and 12, 1858; the *New-York Herald*, Oct. 6 and 13, 1858; and the *Brooklyn Daily Eagle*, Oct. 6, 7, 1858. For a sample of national grieving over the loss of the Crystal Palace, see also *Scientific American*, Oct. 16, 1858; *The Spirit of the Times*, Oct. 30, 1858; *Chicago Press and Tribune*, Oct 6, 7, 1858; *Daily Columbus Enquirer*, Oct. 7, 1858; *The Farmer's Cabinet* (Amherst, NH), Oct. 13, 1858; *German Reformed Messenger* (Philadelphia), Oct. 13, 1858; *Hartford Daily Courant*, Oct. 6, 1858; *Memphis Daily Appeal*, Oct. 9, 1858; *San Antonio Ledger*, Oct. 16, 1858; *The Weekly Wisconsin Patriot*, Oct. 9, 23, 1858; and the *American Phrenological Journal,* Nov. 1858. Estimates of the number of people inside at the time of the fire varied from 1,000 to 3,000.

2. Diary of Morgan Dix, the Archives of Trinity Church, New York. My thanks to Don Gerardi for bringing this source to my attention. Cf. Allan Nevins and Milton Halsey Thomas (eds.), *The Diary of George Templeton Strong*, 4 vols. (New York, 1952), II, 416; and *First Impressions of the New World on Two Travellers from the Old* (London, 1859), 97–98. Sunset that day was at 5:32 p.m. U.S. Naval Observatory, Astronomical Applications Department, at http://aa.usno.navy.mil/rstt/onedaytable?.

3. https://www.measuringworth.com.

4. George S. Baxter to _____ Hawkins, Oct. 7, 1858: N-YHS, CPP, Box 48B; Frank H. Biglow to Elizabeth Biglow, Oct. 7, 1858: MCNY, Manuscripts and Ephemera, 47.93.

One: Glances at Europe

1. Greeley, *Recollections of a Busy Life* (New York, 1869), 268–71; Greeley, *Glances at Europe*, 3rd ed. (New York, 1852), 2–18; Foster Rhea Dulles, *Americans Abroad: Two Centuries of European Travel* (Ann Arbor, MI, 1964), 47–49; Allison Lockwood, *Passionate Pilgrims: The American Traveler in Great Britain, 1800–1914* (Cranbury, NJ, 1981), 150–51. The *Liverpool Mercury*, April 29, 1851, reports the arrival of the *Baltic* in that port. On railway accidents in England, which are "becoming more numerous than ever," see *New-York Daily Times*, Oct. 6, 1851.

2. Michael Leapman, *The World for a Shilling: How the Great Exhibition of 1851 Shaped a Nation* (London, 2001), 34; Kenneth Luckhurst, *The Story of Exhibitions* (London, 1951). Also Thomas Gordon Jayne, "The New York Crystal Palace: An International Exhibition of Goods and Ideas," unpublished M.A. thesis, University of Delaware, May 1990, pp. 1–16.

3. The Exhibition's story has been told often. In addition to Leapman's *World for a Shilling*, among the most readable are Yvonne Ffrench, *The Great Exhibition: 1851* (London, 1951), C. H. Gibbs-Smith, *The Great Exhibition of 1851* (London, 1950), Christopher Hobhouse, *1851 and the Crystal Palace* (New York, 1937), and Asa Briggs, *Iron Bridge to Crystal Palace: Impact and Images of the Industrial Revolution* (London, 1979). Also Robert W. Rydell and Nancy Gwinn (eds.), *Fair Representations: World's Fairs and Modern World* (Amsterdam, 1994); *The Book of Fairs: Materials About World's Fairs, 1834–1916, in the Smithsonian Institution Libraries,* with an introductory essay by Robert W. Rydell (Chicago, 1992); and, most recently, chap. 13 of Gavin Weightman, *The Industrial*

Revolutionaries: The Making of the Modern World, 1776–1914 (New York, 2007). Jeffrey Auerbach, "The Great Exhibition and Historical Memory," in *Britain, the Empire, and the World at the Great Exhibition of 1851*, ed. Jeffrey Auerbach and P. H. Hoffenberg (Aldershot, UK, 2008), 89–112, addresses the many discrepancies between the Exhibition's ostensible purposes and reality. Cf. the letter from W. C. Rives reprinted in the *New-York Daily Times*, Oct. 31, 1851.

4. Greeley, *Glances*, 74. Officially, as reported in the *Tribune* for Mar. 3, 1851, Greeley was one of three men chosen to represent the New York City Mechanics' Institute (the other two being former congressman and tannery owner Zadoc Pratt, president of the Institute, and John H. Bowne). On the democratizing influence attributed to exhibitions in America, see Edward S. Cutler, *Recovering the New: Transatlantic Roots of Modernism* (Lebanon, NH, 2003), 134ff.

5. Greeley, *Recollections*, 269; Greeley, *Glances*, 19; *Harper's New Monthly Magazine*, 2 (April 1851), 584–588; Briggs, *Iron Bridge*, 168–69; Michael R. Katz, "But This Building—What on Earth Is It?" *New England Review* 23 (Winter 2002), 65–77; Katz, "The Russian Response to Modernity: Crystal Palace, Eiffel Tower, Brooklyn Bridge," *Southwest Review* 93 (2008), 44–57. For a concise explanation of its construction, see Folke T. Kihlstedt, "The Crystal Palace," *Scientific American* 251 (Oct. 1, 1984), 132–43. Although conventional wisdom attributes "crystal palace" to the popular periodical *Punch*, an earlier usage has recently been found in *The Leader*, a radical British weekly—perhaps a hint that the nickname might not have been intended favorably at first. See en.wikipedia.org/ wiki/The Crystal Palace (Oct. 2, 2012).

6. On excitement, see, e.g., *Brooklyn Eagle*, Mar. 29, 1851; *New-York Daily Tribune*, Apr. 11, 1850; *American Whig Review* 13 (Feb. 1851), 112; Robert F. Dalzell, *American Participation in the Great Exhibition of 1851* (Amherst, MA, 1960), 33. Also the *Brooklyn Eagle*, Nov. 27, 1850; Jun. 19, 1851; *New-York Daily Tribune*, Nov. 11, 13, and 27, 1850; Jan. 17, 27,

May 1, May 29, and Dec. 8, 1851; *The Farmer's Cabinet* (Amherst, NH), Dec. 19, 1850. See also [Eldon Hall], *A Condensed History of the Origination, Rise, Progress and Completion of the "Great Exhibition of the Industry of All Nations," Held in the Crystal Palace, London* (Redfield, NY, 1852), 67–68, and unpaginated appendix. Hall served as the "conductor and delineator" for Barnum's "moving picture." *New-York Daily Times*, Dec. 1, 1851. Dorothy J. Ernst, "Daniel Wells, Jr.: Wisconsin Commissioner to the Crystal Palace Exhibition of 1851," *Wisconsin Magazine of History* 42 (Summer 1959), 245–46. *New-York Daily Tribune* Mar. 26, 1851.

7. *The Weekly Eagle* (Brattleboro), Feb. 11, 1850; Apr. 7, 1851; *New-York Daily Tribune*, Apr. 26, 1851. On the number of American visitors, see *New-York Daily Tribune*, Jul. 23, 1851, tabulating 5,666 departures from American ports to that point; and Lockwood, *Passionate Pilgrims*, 251. Even in late September, "a large number of Americans" remained in London. *New-York Daily Tribune*, Oct. 24, 1851. For the current value of 1851 dollars, see the Measuring Worth website (http://www.measuringworth.com), which also explains why all such calculations need to be taken with a hefty dose of skepticism. The available data on overseas travel confirm a sharp increase in the number of Americans abroad in the 1850s. Brandon Dupont et al., "The Long-Term Rise in Overseas Travel by Americans, 1820–2000," *Economic History Review* 65 (Feb. 2012), 144–67.

8. Lockwood, *Passionate Pilgrims*, 258. Opposition to the exhibition is discussed at greater length in Leapman, *World for a Shilling*, esp. chap. 3; [Eldon Hall], *Condensed History,* 17. See also Marshall Berman, *All That is Solid Melts into Air: The Experience of Modernity* (New York, 1982), 235–48; and Dalzell, *American Participation*, 10–13. For a rare illustration of American disapproval see *American Whig Review* 13 (Feb. 1851), 113–15.

9. Leapman, *World for a Shilling*, 76. Also Ffrench, *Great Exhibition*, 150–51.

10. Jonathan Sperber, *Karl Marx: A Nineteenth-Century Life* (New York, 2013), esp. chap. 7; Sylvia Nasar, *Grand Pursuit: The Story of Economic Genius* (New York, 2011), 36; There is no evidence that Greeley ever crossed paths with Marx, but Marx was friendly with Richard Henry Dana, Greeley's partner, and a year or two later would be hired by the *Tribune* to report on European affairs.

11. Quoted in Dalzell, *American Participation*, 37.

12. Greeley, *Glances*, 20–21.

13. Greeley, *Glances*, 22–23, 114. Cf. *Recollections*, 273–74, which is rather less strident. Leapman, *World for a Shilling,* esp. 111ff. See also French, *Great Exhibition: 1851;* Gibbs-Smith, *Great Exhibition of 1851;* Hobhouse, *1851 and the Crystal Palace.* Lockwood, *Passionate Pilgrims,* 257–58, and Mulvey, *Anglo-American Landscapes,* 61–62.

14. Greeley, *Glances*, 29, 36–37, 116; *New-York Daily Tribune*, Jan. 25, 1851.

15. Dalzell, *American Participation*, 31, 32–34, 38–40, and 50–51; Greeley, *Glances*, 24–25. The *Herald*'s change of heart may have been prompted by the rumors that large numbers of socialists, Greeley among them, were converging on London to foment revolution. The paper subsequently called Greeley's reporting from the Crystal Palace "about as silly as anything of the kind can be." *Punch* quoted in Weightman, *Industrial Revolutionaries*, 224.

16. Greeley, *Glances*, 287; Greeley, *Recollections*, 273; Rogers, *American Superiority*, 84, 87–89; Ernst, "Wells," 247, 250; Dalzell, *American Participation,* 51; Leapman, *World for a Shilling,* 171–77; *New-York Daily Tribune,* Oct. 24, 1851; [Eldon Hall], *Condensed History,* 40–45.

17. Greeley, *Glances*, 125, 289. One small-town editor believed the Great Exhibition had closed too early, before the United States had a fair

chance to fill up its allotted space—"not with baby jumpers, papers, patent churns, straw cutters and suchlike specimens of the fine arts, but with such handicraft articles as would be calculated to leave a better impression of the skill, taste and genius of this great country." *Grand River Times* (Grand Haven, MI), Aug. 20, 1851.

18. Another group had also started to plan for an industrial fair in the United States. Its key figure was John Jay Smith of Philadelphia, who later claimed that he helped get the London Exposition off the ground in 1850 by promising to buy the whole thing when it closed, building included, take everything to America, and reassemble it on Governors Island. When ill health forced him to step aside, others—presumably Riddle and company—took over the project. Smith, *Recollections of John Jay Smith* (Philadelphia, 1892), 166–77; and a pair of handbills, *Astor-house, New York, February [blank] 1851* (New York, 1851), and *World's Fair in America. Railroad and Steamboat Meeting. . . .* (New York, 1851).

19. William C. Richards (ed.), *Official Catalogue of the New-York Exhibition of the Industry of All Nations* (New York, 1853), 17.

20. For in-depth views of wealth and poverty during the great boom, which was not confined to New York, see Eric Hobsbawm, *The Age of Capital, 1848–1875* (New York, 1975); Edward Pessen, *Riches, Class, and Power Before the Civil War* (New York, 1972); Edward K. Spann, *The New Metropolis: New York City, 1840–1857* (New York, 1981); Edwin G. Burrows and Mike Wallace, *Gotham: A History of New York City to 1898* (New York, 1998); David M. Scobey, *Empire City: The Making and Meaning of the New York City Landscape* (Philadelphia, 2002).

21. Charles Hirschfeld, "America on Exhibition: The New York Crystal Palace," *American Quarterly,* 9 (Summer 1959), 101–16; *New-York Daily Times*, Dec. 26, 1851, and Jan. 31, 1852; Jun 6, 1853; *Scientific American*, Dec. 6, 1851, Jan. 3, 1852. Cf. *MADISON Square* [A report adverse to

the Crystal Palace being erected there] (New York, 1852) and Linda Hyman, *Crystal Palace/42nd St./1853–54* (New York, 1974), unpaginated exhibition catalogue. See also *Official Catalogue of the New-York Exhibition,* 11. P. T. Barnum later claimed that Riddle had tried to recruit him as well. Barnum, *The Life of P.T. Barnum, Written by Himself* (London. 1855), 386.

22. *New-York Daily Times*, Mar. 25, 1853; for Franconi's ostrich, see *Barre Patriot*, May 6, 1853.

23. The eleven directors were also named as shareholders of the Association, along with Charles King (President of Columbia University), Edward K. Collins (founder of the Collins Line of steamships), William C. Bryant, August Belmont, Watts Sherman, and William Kent (an attorney and son of the great jurist James Kent).

24. *Scientific American,* Jan. 3, Jun. 26, 1852; Jayne, "New York Crystal Palace," 59–60; *Richmond Inquirer* quoted in the Wilmington, NC, *Journal,* Sept. 2, 1854.

25. There is no evidence that either Carstensen or Gildemeister ever saw the London Crystal Palace in person, but they were quite familiar with Paxton's work inasmuch as the structure they intended for Reservoir Square—notwithstanding their professions of originality for its design—employed similar elements and construction methods. Geo. Carstensen and Chs. Gildemeister, *New York Crystal Palace. Illustrated Description of the Building* (New York, 1854), 47. Full plans for Paxton's Crystal Palace in New York appeared in the London papers almost immediately. They inspired William Dargan, the Irish railroad magnate, to build an iron and glass crystal palace for an industrial exhibition in Dublin. He hired an architect, put up £100,000 of his own money, and opened in May 1853. Carstensen and Gildemeister were aware of his project, but how much they knew remains unclear. *Siobhán Kilfeather, Dublin: A Cultural History* (New York, 2005), 143–44. Reservoir Square "is a

spot without any physical recommendation," agreed *The Illustrated Magazine of Art,* 2 (1853), 250.

26. Georg Carstensen and Chas. Gildemeister, *New York Crystal Palace: Illustrated Description* (New York, 1854), 48.

27. *New-York Daily Times*, Oct. 13, 31, 1852.

Two: An Honor to the Country

1. *Scientific American,* Nov. 6, 1852; *New-York Daily Times,* Jul. 13, 15, 1853. As reported in the same paper on Jul. 22, the Crystal Palace eventually got is own fire department as well—a pair of superintendents, their four assistants, an "elegant and powerful" fire engine parked permanently under the dome, and an abundance of hydrants, hoses, and water buckets, plus two huge storage tanks. Thus, the building enjoys "complete protection" from fire.

2. Foster, *Fifteen Minutes Around New York* (New York, 1856), 11. *Fifteen Minutes* was first published in early 1853. Foster's work is discussed Stuart M. Blumin, "Explaining the New Metropolis: Perception, Depiction, and Analysis in Mid-Nineteenth-Century New York City," *Journal of Urban History* 11 (Nov. 1984), 9–38; and "George G. Foster and the Emerging Metropolis," in *New York by Gas-Light and Other Urban Sketches by George G. Foster*, ed. Stuart M. Blumin (Berkeley, 1990), 1–61. Also George R. Taylor, "Gaslight Foster: A New York 'Journeyman Journalist' at Mid Century," *NYH* 58 (Jul. 1977), 297–312. Detmold later claimed that he made the men work at night, too. *Scientific American*, Sept. 24, 1853.

3. *New-York Daily Times,* Nov. 1, 1852, Jan. 5, 18, Mar. 10, 25, Jul. 15, 16, 28, 1853; *New-York Daily Tribune,* Oct, 26, Nov. 1, 13, 20, 1852; Brooklyn *Eagle*, Apr. 5, 1853; *Family Circle* quoted in the *Barre Patriot,* Feb. 4, 1853. The *Home Journal* quoted in the *Farmer's Cabinet,* Jul. 7, 1853. *Scientific American*, Aug. 27, 1853; the *Constitution*, Jul. 20, 1853. Cf.

Putnam's Monthly, 2 (Jul.–Dec. 1853), 125, on the "mammoth shanties" in the vicinity. Also Jayne, "New York Crystal Palace," 59–62; and Earle E. Coleman, "The Exhibition in the Palace: A Bibliographical Essay," *Bulletin of the New York Public Library* 64 (September 1960), 459–77.

4. *Statement Made by the Association for the Exhibition of the Industry of All Nations in Regards to the Organization and Progress of the Enterprise* (New York, [1853]); *Scientific American,* Jun. 26, Oct. 23, 1852. The unauthorized engraving infuriated Sedgwick and triggered an exchange of recriminations in which each side accused the other of hypocrisy and money-grubbing. *New-York Daily Tribune*, Nov. 23, Dec. 4, 6, 9, 1852; *New-York Daily Times*, Oct. 25, Dec.10, 15, 1852. In November of that year, the Association came out with its own engraving and insisted that *Scientific American*'s animosity stemmed from "personal resentment." *Scientific American*, Apr. 2, 1853. William G. Le Duc, "Minnesota at the Crystal Palace Exhibition, New York, 1853," *Minnesota History Bulletin* 1 (Aug. 1916), 351–68. For a glowing report on Le Duc's activities, see *New-York Daily Tribune*, Aug. 16, 1853.

5. Carstensen and Gildemeister, *New York Crystal Palace,* 11. The *New-York Daily Times* for Jul. 15, 1853, put the total area of the ground floor and gallery at just under 249,700 square feet, or 5.7 acres. Greeley, *Art and Industry*, 14, gives the area of the main building as 173,000 square feet and that of the annex as 33,000 square feet, for a total of 206,000 in all, or 4.7 acres.

6. On the rise in iron prices, see *Scientific American*, Feb. 5, 1853. Greenough was friendly with John M. Batchelder, a member of the Board from Massachusetts.

7. Carstensen and Gildemeister, *New York Crystal Palace*, 9–22; *Harper's New Monthly Magazine* 11 (Nov. 1853). The phrase that begins with "stood honored" comes from a letter by "A Looker-On" in the *New-York Daily Times*, Jul. 20, 1853. It is almost certainly the work of Carstensen.

Cf. the letter from Gildemeister, as well as the one from both him and Carstensen, *New-York Daily Tribune,* Jul. 23, 30, 1853. Superintendent Du Pont also had run-ins with the Board and quit in the autumn of 1853. See Kevin J. Weddle, *Lincoln's Tragic Admiral: The Life of Samuel Francis Du Pont* (Charlottesville, VA, 2005), 57–58.

8. The charter of incorporation allowed the Associates to issue more stock if necessary. They did so on two subsequent occasions, doubling the number of $100 shares to 4,000.

9. See their letter to the editor, *New-York Daily Times,* Jul. 29, 1853. For the Board's position, see their pamphlet, issued in the spring of that year, *Statement Made by the Association for the Exhibition of the Industry of All Nations, In Regard to the Organization and Progress of the Enterprise* (New York, 1853). Greeley, *Art and Industry as Represented in the Exhibition at the Crystal Palace, New York—1853–4* (New York, 1853), 27. Cf. *Scientific American*, Jul. 23, 1853. When the contractors and mechanics he had hired honored him with a lavish banquet at the Astor House, Detmold himself twisted the knife in a speech charging again that the architects failed to deliver necessary drawings on time. He even commandeered credit for choosing their design to begin with. *New-York Daily Times*, Sept. 14, 1853: *New-York Daily Tribune*, Sept. 14, 15, 1853.

10. The notice of Mary Carstensen's death appears in the *New York Times*, Dec. 17, 1880. For Georg Cartensen, see *Scientific American*, Feb. 21, 1857; also Richard Swett, "Georg Carstensen and the New York Crystal Palace," *Leadership by Design* (Atlanta, 2005), 25–30. For Detmold's obituary, see *New York Times*, Jul. 5, 1887.

11. *Scientific American*, Jun. 4, 1853; *New-York Daily*, Mar., 25, 1853. Latting's only claim to fame thus far seems to be the patent he won in 1843 (US 3346A) for improvements in the design of umbrellas. *New-York Daily Tribune* for July 22, 1841, reported that a schoolteacher named "Warring"

Latting had been arrested for fraud, but whether that was simply a misprint cannot be determined. For an account of the July 1 storm, see the *New-York Daily Tribune*, Jul. 2, 1853.

12. The Latting Obervatory bears a striking resemblance to the derricks that sprouted up only a few years later in the oil fields of western Pennsylvania. As it happens, the inventor of the oil derrick was a New York lawyer named George Henry Bissell, who may have learned a thing or two by studying the construction of Latting's Observatory. Bissell got confirmation of oil's profitability, moreover, from Benjamin Silliman, the Yale chemist and a sometime trustee of the Crystal Palace Association.

13. For a description of how the Latting Observatory was built, consult *The Plough, the Loom, and the Anvil* (Nov. 1853), 312–14. Also Lee E. Gray, *From Ascending Rooms to Express Elevators: A History of Passenger Elevator in the 19th Century* (Mobile, AL, 2002), 24–26; and Andreas Bernard, *Lifted: A Cultural History of the Elevator* (New York, 2014). On the Drummond light and telescope, see the *New-York Daily Tribune,* Jul. 6, 1853; *Daily New-York Times*, Jul. 27, 1853. In April, concerns about the observatory's safety prompted an inspection tour by the grand jury, which assured the public that the tower was being built upon "correct principles." Ibid., Apr. 25, 1853. Latting's plans for steam elevators are described in the *New-York Daily Times*, Mar. 25, 1853. Lithography is covered in John W. Reps, *Views and Viewmakers of Urban America* (Columbia, MO, 1984) and *Bird's Eye Views: Historic Lithographs of North American Cities* (New York, 1998). The only photo of the observatory known to survive was taken by Victor Prevost (Figure 2.16). See Julie Melby, "Victor Prevost: Painter, Lithographer, Photographer," *History of Photography* 35 (August 2011): 221–39; Jeff L. Rosenheim, " 'A Palace for the Sun': Early Photography in New York City," in *Art and the Empire City: New York, 1825–1861*, ed. Catherine

H. Voorsanger and John K. Howat (New York, 2000), 226–41; and Virginia Fister, "From the Second Empire to the Empire City: Victor Prevost's Architectural Views, 1854–1856," online essay for the Bard Graduate Center exhibition *Visualizing 19th-Century New York,* David Jaffe (cur.), 2014, http://visualizingnyc.org/about/.

14. Quoted in the *Ohio State Journal*, Jul. 19, 1853. See also the similarly rapturous verdict in Humphrey Phelps*, The Lions of New York: Being a Guide to Objects of Interest in and Around the Great Metropolis* (New York, 1853), 12.

15. *New-York Daily Times,* Jul. 1, 14, 1853.

16. *United States Review* 33 (Jul. 1853), 92; *New-York Daily Times*, Jul. 12, 13, 14, 15, 19, 1853; *New-York Daily Tribune*, Jul. 2, 12, 13, 14, 1853; *Harper's New Monthly Magazine* 6 (May 1853), 7 (Jun. 1853); *Scientific American*, Jun. 4, Aug. 27, 1853; "Letters from New York," *Southern Literary Messenger* XIX (Aug. 1853), 510–13. *Putnam's Monthly* 2 (Dec. 1853), 377.

17. *New-York Daily Times,* Jul. 13, 1853.

18. *Scientific American*, Jul. 30, 1853; *New-York Daily Times*, Jul. 9, 15, 1853; the latter issue also included a note that two street railway lines alone brought 44,000 passengers up to Reservoir Square that day, while thousands more came by other means. *New-York Daily Tribune*, Jul. 15, 1853; "Letters from New York," *Southern Literary Messenger.* Greeley, *Art and Industry*, 17–19.

19. Pierce's trip to New York and the opening-day hoopla were thoroughly covered in the *New-York Daily Times*, July 13, 14, 15, and 16, 1853, and the *New-York Daily Tribune*, Jul. 14, 15, Aug. 16, 1853. But see also Roy F. Nichols, *Franklin Pierce, Young Hickory of the Granite Hills* (Philadelphia, 1958), 279–82; Brooks McNamara, *Day of Jubilee: The Great Age of Public Celebrations in New York, 1788–1909* (New Brunswick, NJ, 1997), 94–96; and Coleman, "The Exhibition," 459.

20. *New-York Daily Times*, Jul. 15, 28, 1853. Cf. *Putnam's Monthly Magazine* 2 (Jul.-Dec. 1853), 123.

21. B. Silliman Jr. and C. R. Goodrich (eds.), *The World of Science, Art, and Industry, Illustrated from Examples in the New-York Exhibition, 1853– 54* (New York, 1854), 6 (originally issued in parts as *The Illustrated Record of the New York Exhibition of the Industry of All Nations*).

22. Margot Gayle, *Cast-Iron Architecture in New York* (New York, 1974); Carol Gayle and Margot Gayle, "The Emergence of Cast-Iron Architecture in the United States: Defining the Role of James Bogardus," *APT Bulletin* 29, no. 2 (1998), pp. 5–12; Turpin C. Bannister, "Bogardus Revisited. Part II: The Iron Towers," *Journal of the Society of Architectural Historians* 16 (Mar. 1957), 11–19.

23. *United States Democratic Review* 7 (Jul. 1853), 92; *The National Magazine*, 2 (Jan.–Jun. 1853), 80; *Harper's New Monthly Magazine* 7 (Jun. and Nov. 1853); Le Duc, "Minnesota at the Crystal Palace Exhibition"; *Illustrated Magazine of Art* 2 (1853), xxx; Horace Greeley, *New-York Daily Tribune,* Jul. 9, 1853; Nevins and Thomas (eds.), *Diary of Strong*, II, 127. Cf. *Ohio State Journal,* Jan. 3, 1853; *New-York Daily Times*, Jul. 14, 1853; *Putnam's Monthly* 8 (August, 1853), 124–25; and Hirschfeld, "America on Exhibition," 109ff. Also John Loraine Abbott, *The Wonders of the World* (Hartford, CT, 1856), 697–702. Presumably Sedgwick also refused admission to the white, six-foot-tall, 1,800-pound hog sent by steamer from Wisconsin. *New-York Daily Times*, Jun. 4, 1853. For Sam Clemens, see J. R. LeMaster and James D. Wilson (eds.), *The Mark Twain Encyclopedia* (1993), 194.

24. *New-York Daily Times*, Jul. 19, 20, 21, 25; Aug. 2, 6, 8, 19, 23, 1853; *New-York Daily Tribune*, Jul. 15, 16, 18, 19, 22, 1843; *Putnam's Monthly* (Aug. 1853), 126. We know the Crystal Palace had water closets because the *Times* let slip on August 6 that they had been installed—at last. Water closets in the London Crystal Palace were actually discussed more openly. From the West Coast, meanwhile, came word not only

that the Crystal Palace was unfinished, but that "America's Industrial Exhibition, which was to eclipse royalty, is nothing more than a Wall Street stock jobbing enterprise." *Alta California*, Aug. 1, 1853. See *New-York Daily Tribune*, Sept. 20, 1853 and *Harper's New Monthly Magazine* (Nov. 1853), 848, on the fluctuations of Crystal Palace stock.

25. The Exhibition's influence on Whitman's poetry is discussed in Edward S. Cutler, *Recovering the New: Transatlantic Roots of Modernism* (Hanover, NH, 2003) and Paul Benton, "Whitman, Christ, and the Crystal Palace Police," *Walt Whitman Quarterly Review* 17 (Spring 2000), 147–65. Also Cutler, "Passage to Modernity: Leaves of Grass and the 1853 Crystal Palace Exhibition in New York," *Walt Whitman Quarterly Review* 16 (Fall 1998), 65–89. Whitman's "Song of the Exhibition," a poem sometimes said to be about the 1853 Crystal Palace, was in fact commissioned for the 1870 show of the American Institute. For the visitor from Illinois, see John Reynolds, *Sketches of the Country on the Northern Route from Belleville, Illinois, to the City of New York, and Back by the Ohio Valley, Together with a Glance at the Crystal Palace* (Belleville, IL, 1854), 187. Fifty years later, another visitor, Henry James, still remembered being deeply impressed by Thorvaldsen's "enormous" group. James, *A Small Boy and Others* (New York, 1913), 169–70. Hirschfeld, "America on Exhibition," 108, puts the total number of paying visitors at 1 million.

26. John F. Watson, *Historic Tales of Olden Time: Concerning the Early Settlement and Advancement of New-York City and State* (New York, 1832), 204–7; Richard Gassan, "The First American Tourist Guidebooks," *Book History* 8 (2005), 51–75; Gassan, *The Birth of American Tourism: New York, the Hudson Valley, and American Culture, 1790–1830* (Amherst, MA, 2008); Catherine Cocks, *Doing the Town: The Rise of Urban Tourism in the United States, 1859–1915* (Berkeley, CA, 2001), 1–40; Barbara Penner, *Newlyweds on Tour: Honeymooning in*

Nineteenth-Century America (Durham, NH, 2009), esp. 125–37; Richard Plunz, "City: Culture: Nature: The New York Wilderness and the Urban Sublime," in *The Urban Lifeworld: Formation, Perception, Representation*, ed. Peter Madsen and Richard Plunz (London, 2002), 45–76; John F. Sears, *Sacred Places: American Tourist Attractions in the Nineteenth Century* (New York, 1989).

27. James Robertson, *A Few Months in America* (London, 1855), 18; Ellen W. Kramer, "Contemporary Descriptions of New York City and Its Public Architecture ca. 1850," *Journal of the Society of Architectural Historians* 27 (Dec. 1968), 264–80; Meryle R. Evans, "Knickerbocker Hotels and Restaurants, 1800–1850," *New-York Historical Society Quarterly* 36 (Oct. 1952), 376–409; "Lord Acton's American Diaries," 730; Ivan D. Steen, "Palaces for Travelers: New York City Hotels in the 1850's As Viewed by British Visitors," *New York History* 51 (Apr. 1970), 269–86. Winston Weisman, "Commercial Palaces of New York: 1845–1875," *The Art Bulletin* 36 (Dec. 1954), 285–302; *Putnam's Monthly* 2 (Feb. 1853), 122. Old prejudices died hard. Cf. Anthony Trollope's 1862 verdict that "In other large cities, cities as large in name as New York, there are works of art, fine buildings, ruins, ancient churches, picturesque costumes, and the tombs of celebrated men. But in New York there are none of these things." Quoted in Shaun O'Connell, *Remarkable, Unspeakable New York: A Literary History* (Boston, 1995), 13.

28. Foster, *Fifteen Minutes*, 8; *New-York Daily Times*, May 20, 1853; Jun. 18, 1856.

29. *Putnam's Monthly* 2 (Dec. 1853), 577–78; *New-York Daily Times*, Mar. 31, 1853; and the *Sunday Albany Atlas*, Mar. 27, 1853, quoted in Jayne, "New York Crystal Palace," 60. Cf. [William Bobo], *Glimpses of New-York City* (Charleston, SC, 1852), which is intended for every class of traveler to the city *except* tourists. A planter from Columbus,

Mississippi, encountered no fewer then thirty people from the same town when he arrived in New York for the grand opening of the Crystal Palace. John Hope Franklin, *A Southern Odyssey*, 15–16, 33–35, 42, 89, 174–75; also Philip S. Foner, *Business and Slavery* (New York, 1941).

The old Jeffersonian animus against cities, though weakened by the growth of urban tourism, would still exert a powerful influence on the attitudes of many Americans. See Thomas Bender, *Toward an Urban Vision: Ideas and Institutions in Nineteenth Century America* (Baltimore, 1975).

30. Humphrey Phelps*, Lions of New York*, 12. The "Park" Phelps refers to is now City Hall Park. Gunther Barth, "Demopiety: Speculations on Urban Beauty, Western Scenery, and the Discovery of the American Cityscape," *Pacific Historical Review* 52 (1983), 249–66.

31. *New-York Daily Times*, Jul. 14, 1853.

32. *New-York Daily Times*, Jul. 21, 1853; Foster, *Fifteen Minutes*, 11; *Putnam's Monthly* 2 (Dec. 1853), 582; *The Living Age* 40 (Jan. 14, 1854), 111.

33. Even after it had opened, however, people still complained that the displays of minerals remained unarranged and often unidentified, and that no catalogue had as yet appeared. See Daniel E. Russell, "Crystals at the Crystal Palace: The Mineralogical Display at the 1853 Crystal Palace Exhibit in New York City," http://mindat.org/article .php/196/ (Jan. 22, 2017).

34. *Scientific American*, Feb. 25, 1854. *New-York Daily Times*, Jan. 23, Feb. 11, 25, 1854; *New-York Daily Tribune,* Feb. 21, 1854; *The Daily Atlas* (Boston), Jan. 20, 1854; and the *Brooklyn Daily Eagle*, Feb. 13, 1854. In fairness, the Exhibition also faced competition, most notably from the Woman's Rights Convention that opened in the city in September 1853. A spirited argument for keeping the building as a permanent— but national—exhibition hall is in the *Tribune*, Nov. 10, 1853. "$13.9 million" is in 2015 dollars, as calculated by measuringworth.com. Other methods of computation yield substantially higher figures. It may

be worth noting that the Crystal Palace wasn't the most costly construction project in the pre–Civil War era. The Erie Canal, for example, cost 7 million in 1825 dollars—a sum now equivalent to around $170 million. *New-York Daily Times*, Aug. 19, 1853.

Three: The Wilderness of Objects

1. Prince Albert's initial plan was to facilitate comparisons by displaying similar items side by side, irrespective of origin, but that never happened because each country preferred that its contributions be seen together. The odd juxtaposition of objects that resulted is described in Leapman, *World for a Shilling*, 130ff. Almost from the outset, the New York Association seems to have reconciled itself to the inevitability of a similar approach.

2. William C. Richards, *A Day in The New York Crystal Palace, and How to Make the Most of It* (New York, 1853), 94–95. Richards and the other contributors to the catalogue thought it "unadvisable" to classify some contributions, such as the wax figurines of Mexican tortilla bakers. *Official Catalogue of the New-York Exhibition* (New York, 1853), 191; Sillliman and Goodrich, *World of Science*, 44.

3. In his *Illustrated History of the Hat* (New York, 1848), 41, Genin argued that "The latest fashion is always the best, because it is of necessity an improvement on the one which it supplants; therefore, to rail at an existing fashion is simply to rail at improvement." It was a line of reasoning that must have endeared him to the Association.

4. Horace Greeley, *Art and Industry, as Represented in the Exhibition at the Crystal Palace, New York 1853–4, Showing the Progress and State of the Various Useful and Esthetic Pursuits* (New York, 1853), ix, xxiii; *New-York Daily Tribune*, Sept. 28, 1853; *New-York Daily Times*, Jun. 4, Jul. 21, 22, Aug. 4, 1853; *Scientific American*, Aug. 27, 1853; *Illustrated Magazine of Art* 2 (1853), 258; *Southern Literary Messenger* 20 (Jan.

1854), 29–30. *Scientific American*, Oct. 8, 1853, later grumbled that the Exhibition favored "soap-chandlers and confectioners, and patent medicine brokers, and gew-gaw manufacturers" over authentic industrialists. See also John Reynolds*, Sketches of the Country on the Northern Route from Belleville, Illinois, to the City of New York, and Back by the Ohio Valley, Together with a Glance at the Crystal Palace* (Belleville, IL, 1854), 192.

5. Greeley, *Art and Industry*, 69–70, 91, 203; the *Tribune* subsequently informed readers that all exhibits had finally received suitable identification, but the paper continued to complain about poor lighting. The *Times* said that even with gas lighting, the Picture Gallery was too "dim." It also found that many objects were incorrectly classified to begin with and pronounced the official catalogue "almost useless." *The New-York Daily Times*, Jul. 22, Aug. 4, 26, 30, 1853. Cf. similar protests in *Scientific American*, Aug. 27, 1853; and C. R. Goodrich (ed.), *Science and Mechanism: As Illustrated in the New York Exhibition, 1853–4* (New York, 1854), v.

6. *Putnam's Monthly* 2 (Aug. 1853), 126; Richards, *A Day in The New York Crystal Palace,* 107; Greeley, *Art and Industry*, 299–300. Whitney's gin had been around since 1793, Silliman and Goodrich agreed, but as a "peculiarly national" invention and a "cornerstone" of American industry, it still held great interest. *Science, Art, and Industry,* 6. The Crystal Palace wasn't a museum, nonetheless, and this kind of reasoning, though rare, marked a further retreat from the promise to be more selective than the London show.

7. Richards, *A Day in The New York Crystal Palace,* 107–12; Greeley, *Art and Industry*, 299; Silliman and Goodrich, *Science, Art, and Industry*, 6.

8. Richards, *A Day in The New York Crystal Palace*, 110, 112–15; Greeley, *Art and Industry*, 298. But see *The Illustrated Magazine of Art* 2 (1853), 262, which found the Machine Arcade disappointing.

9. *New-York Daily Tribune*, Nov. 10, 1853; Coleman, "The Exhibition," 468–70. The same thing happens even today. See, e.g., Cutler, *Recovering the New*, 137.

10. No doubt some Americans still used "art" in the old-fashioned way, as a synonym for "skill" (or "artistry," as we would say nowadays). Nonetheless, the transformation of the term into a distinct category of aesthetics, not to say commerce, had been well under way since the 17th century.

11. Silliman and Goodrich, *Science, Art, and Industry*, 185–86; Catherine H. Voorsanger, "'Gorgeous Articles of Furniture': Cabinetmaking in the Empire City," in *Art and the Empire City: New York, 1825–1861*, ed. Catherine H. Voorsanger and John K. Howat (New York, 2000), 287–325.

12. H. W. Bellows, *The Moral Significance of the Crystal Palace* (New York, 1853), 11–14, 16–18. On the elite's pursuit of luxury in the 1850s, see Burrows and Wallace, *Gotham*, 712–34.

13. *New-York Daily Tribune*, July 14, 1853; Silliman and Goodrich, *Science, Art, and Industry*, 29.

14. [Lewis Tappan], *The Fugitive Slave Bill: Its History and Unconstitutionality, with An Account of the Seizure and Enslavement of James Hamlet* (New York, 1850); Richard Hofstadter and Michael Wallace (eds.), *American Violence: a Documentary History* (New York, 1970), 309–12; Sean Wilentz, *Chants Democratic: New York City and the Rise of the American Working Class, 1788–1850* (New York, 1984), esp. 363–389; Paul Gilje, *Rioting in America* (Bloomington, 1996), esp. 69–70; Edward L. Widmer, *Young America: The Flowering of Democracy in New York City* (New York, 1999); Spann, *New Metropolis*, 235–39: Burrows and Wallace, *Gotham*, 761–65; Peter G. Buckley, "To the Opera House: Culture and Society in New York City, 1820–1860," unpub. Ph.D. dissertation, Stony Brook University, 1984. William G. Le Duc, "Minnesota at the Crystal Palace Exhibition," 364. It is worth

noting that Carstensen and Gildemeister dedicated their book on the Crystal Palace to their "fellow-laborers… the artists and artisans of the United States." This may have something to do with their shabby treatment by the Crystal Palace Association.

15. *New-York Daily Times*, Jan. 28, Mar. 9, 20, May 13, Jul. 2, 27, Aug. 16, 19, 28, Sept. 13, Oct. 4, 12, 13, 23, 28, Nov. 22, 23, Dec. 4, 1852. *New-York Daily Tribune*, Jan. 2, 3, Jun. 1, 2, 16, 30, Jul. 5, 28, 29, Aug. 13, 16, 18, Sept. 14, 18, Oct. 14, 27, Nov. 22, 23, Dec. 10, 25, 28, 1852. Spann, *New Metropolis*, 390–91.

16. *New-York Daily Times,* Mar. 24, Apr 18, Jun. 22, Jul. 6, Sept. 23, Dec.12, 16, 22, 1853. *New-York Daily Tribune*, Feb. 28, Jun. 23, 24, Jul. 6, Aug. 8, Dec, 12, 1853.

17. The Ladies of the Mission*, The Old Brewery, and the New Mission House at the Five Points* (New York, 1854), 290–99.

18. *New-York Daily Times*, Jul. 22, 1853; *New-York Daily Tribune*, Sept. 28, 1853. Cf. *Putnam's Monthly* 2 (Dec. 1853), 580, 582.

19. *New-York Daily Tribune*, Jul. 30, Aug. 17, 1853; *New-York Daily Times*, Aug. 17, 1853. In the New York Crystal Palace, according to Horace Greeley, so many people surrounded both works that they were hard to see. *Art and Industry*, 57; cf. the *New-York Daily Times*, Aug. 19, 1853.

20. I have made liberal use here of Joy S. Kasson, *Marble Queens and Captives: Women in Nineteenth-Century American Sculpture* (New Haven, CT, 1990). Also helpful were Linda Hyman, "The *Greek Slave* By Hiram Powers: High Art as Popular Culture," *Art Journal* 35 (Spring 1976), 216–23; Vivien Green, "Hiram Powers's *Greek Slave*: Emblem of Freedom," *The American Art Journal* 14 (Autumn 1982), 31–39; David Scobey, "Nymphs and Satyrs: Sex and the Bourgeois Public Sphere in Victorian New York," *Winterthur Portfolio* 3 (Spring 2002), 43–66; and Thayer Tolles, "Modeling a Reputation: The American Sculptor and New York City," in *Art and the Empire City:*

New York, 1825–1861, ed. Catherine H. Voorsanger and John K. Howat (New York, 2000), 135–67.

21. *Putnam's Monthly* 2 (Aug. 1853), 126; 2 (Dec. 1853), 580; Greeley, *Art and Industry*, 55. He also pronounced Powers's work adept but derivative. For a similar judgment, see Goodrich, *Science and Mechanism*, 254. Interestingly, in 1847 the *Tribune* had praised the *Greek Slave* "as the greatest work of modern sculpture." *New-York Daily Tribune*, Aug. 26, 1847; *New-York Daily Times*, Feb. 28, 1854. When medals were handed out, however, Powers came away with only an honorable mention for the *Greek Slave* and his other work. *Brooklyn Daily Eagle*, Jan. 28, 1854. Mostly, this outcome was ridiculed, but on February 18, 1854, the *Poughkeepsie Journal* expressed its approval, saying the Association was wrong to have let "the vile statuary into the Palace at all," inasmuch as it was "obscene" and "an insult to the moral sensibilities of the community."

22. *New-York Daily Times,* Feb. 11, 1854.

23. *New-York Daily Tribune*, Mar. 1, 7, 1854; *New-York Daily Times*, Feb. 25, 28, 1854.

24. Bluford Adams*, E Pluribus Barnum: The Great Showman and the Making of U.S. Popular Culture* (Minneapolis, 1997), 88–90; *Scientific American*, Apr. 22, 1854.

25. *New-York Daily Tribune*, Mar. 1, 1854.

26. *New-York Daily Tribune*, Mar. 10, 1854; Barnum, *Life*, 387. On the Board's first ballot, Barnum received the votes of just seven of the sixteen members present—not exactly a groundswell of support.

27. *New-York Daily Times,* Mar. 30, Apr. 6, 27, 1854; *New-York Daily Tribune*, Apr. 3, 17, 21, 27, 29, 1854; *Brooklyn Daily Eagle*, Apr. 11, 1854; Barnum, *Life*, 387.

28. *New-York Daily Times,* Mar. 22, Apr. 7, 17, 1854, Jan. 24, 1855; for Munn's side of the story, see *Scientific American*, 9 (Mar. 25, 1854), 229.

29. *New-York Daily Times*, Mar. 20, 1854. For the full report, see Sir Charles Lyell, *New York Industrial Exhibition* (London, 1854).

30. My account of the re-inauguration was assembled from the *Brooklyn Daily Eagle*, May 4, 1854; plus coverage published on May 5, 1854, by the *New-York Daily Times*, the *New-York Daily Tribune*, the *Daily Atlas* (Boston) and the *Pittsfield (MA) Sun,* May 11, 1854. The *Tribune's* coverage was reprinted in *How To See the New York Crystal Palace: Being A Concise Guide to the Principal Objects in the Exhibition As Remodeled, 1854* (New York, 1854). Also E. H. Chapin, *The American Idea, and What Grows Out of It: An Oration, Delivered in the New-York Crystal Palace, July 4, 1854* (Boston, 1854).

31. *Daily Atlas*, Jun. 10, 12, 1854; *Pittsfield Sun*, Jun.15, 1854; *Brooklyn Daily Eagle*, Jun. 23, 1854; *Ohio State Journal*, Jun. 28, 1854; *Scientific American*, Jul. 30, 1853.

32. *New York Daily Tribune*, May 30, 1854; *Scientific American*, Nov. 25, 1854. For some trenchant observations on the Otis legend, see Andreas Bernard, *Lifted: A Cultural History of the Elevator* (New York, 2014).

33. *New-York Daily Times*, Jul. 13, 1854. Neil Harris, *Humbug: The Art of P.T. Barnum* (Chicago, 1973), 147–48, *Scientific American,* Jul. 22, 1854.

34. *Harper's* 8 (April, 1854), 695; *The Farmer's Cabinet*, Aug. 24, 1854; *Ohio State Journal*, Aug. 16, Nov. 8, 1854; *Pittsfield Sun*, Nov. 23, 1854; *Barre Patriot,* Nov. 24, 1854. The Crystal Palace Association was officially in receivership before the end of the year, but disgruntled exhibitors were still clamoring for the return of their property. *Scientific American*, Jun. 9, 1855. *New-York Daily Tribune*, Apr. 19, 1855; *New-York Daily Times*, Apr. 20, 1855.

Four: The Widowed Bride of Sixth Avenue

1. *New-York Daily Times*, Jan. 24, Mar. 22, Apr. 20, 25, Jun. 1, 6, Nov. 16, 1855, Sept. 1, 1856; *Putnam's* 10 (Jul. 1857), 135; *New-York Daily Tribune*, Mar. 17, 23, 1855. Burrows and Wallace, *Gotham*, 834–35.

2. The judgment against Barnum was the equivalent of around $430,000 in 2014 dollars. The following August, Barnum's creditors, not including Munn, forced him to auction off a substantial quantity of assets to pay additional judgments against him. *New-York Daily Times*, Aug. 6, 1856.

3. *New-York Daily Times*, Jun. 30, Aug 9, 1855. *Description of the Mammoth Tree from California, Now Erected at the Crystal Palace, Sydenham* (London, [1857]) has numerous extracts from the contemporary preiss in Britain, America, and elsewhere. In time, conservationists came to cite the destruction of this and other redwoods for exhibition as acts of appalling vandalism. See, e.g., Gifford Pinchot, *A Short Account of the Big Trees of California* (Washington, DC, 1900).

4. *New-York Daily Times*, Sept. 28 1855.

5. *New-York Daily Times,* Sept. 7, 1855, Sept. 5, Oct. 4, 1856.

6. *New-York Daily Tribune*, Apr. 20, 27, May 3, 10, Nov. 8, 1854; *New-York Daily Times*, Aug, 11, 1854; Jul. 24, 1855; *Scientific American,* Nov. 13, 1852, blamed the limited space in Castle Garden for the chaotic arrangement of exhibits there.

7. *Transactions of the American Institute of the City of New-York* (Albany, 1855), 8; *New-York Daily Times*, Oct. 1, 18, 30, 1855; *New-York Daily Tribune*, Aug. 10, Oct.13, 19, 22, 26, Nov. 1, 1855. The Institute did not publish a catalogue of exhibits or a list of the awards it handed out, a subject of frequent complaint. *New-York Daily Times*, Nov. 15, 19, 1855.

8. *New-York Daily Times*, Jan. 4, 1856, Sept. 18, 26, 1857.

9. *New-York Daily Times*, May 9, 1856. A couple of weeks later, the Council received a petition from 635 residents of the neighborhood urging it not to renew the lease. In light of such widespread unhappiness with the Crystal Palace, Banks cannot be dismissed as simply a solitary crank. *New-York Daily Times*, May 21, 1856.

10. *New-York Daily Times*, Sept. 1, 3, 1856; *New-York Daily Tribune*, Sept. 1, 1856; *New York Herald*, Aug. 31, 1856; *Brooklyn Eagle*, Aug. 30, 1856; *Boston Daily Atlas*, Sept. 1, 1856.

11. *New York Herald*, Nov. 19, 1856; *New-York Daily Tribune*, Feb, 19, Mar. 17, 1857. Barnum quoted in Jayne, "New York Crystal Palace," 82.

12. *Putnam's Monthly* 9 (Mar. 1857), 336; *New-York Daily Times*, May 1, 28, Jul. 21, Aug. 29, 1857; Mar. 18, 1858; *New-York Daily Tribune*, Aug. 31, 1858.

13. *New-York Daily Times,* Jun. 5, 8, 12, 24, Sept. 25, 1854.

14. *New-York Daily Times*, Dec. 18, 1856; Jun. 17, 1857; Spann, *New Metropolis*, 392–93; Burrows and Wallace, *Gotham*, 838–39.

15. *New-York Daily Times,* Jun. 17, Jul. 5, 6, 7, 8, 1857.

16. James L. Huston, *The Panic of 1857 and the Coming of the Civil War* (Baton Rouge, LA, 1978); Burrows and Wallace, *Gotham*, 842–51.

17. *New-York Daily Times*, Mar. 18, 31, 1858; *New-York Daily Tribune,* Apr. 2, 7, 1858*; New York Herald,* Apr. 12, 1858. The society was named in honor of the mayor of Norfolk, Virginia, who died helping his constituents during a recent yellow fever epidemic.

18. *New-York Daily Times*, Sept. 23, Dec. 12, 1857; Mar. 8, Jun. 1, 1858; *New-York Daily Tribune*, Jun. 1, 2, 1858. After the 1858 fire, the city sued to collect the insurance, arguing that it, not the receiver, was the lawful owner of the Crystal Palace. The Superior Court agreed. *New-York Daily Times*, Jan. 23, 1862.

19. *New-York Daily Times*, Aug. 31, Sept. 1, 2, 3, 1858; *New-York Daily Tribune,* Sept. 2, 3, 1858; McNamara, *Day of Jubilee*, 96–99; Burrows and Wallace, *Gotham*, 675–76. Also http://atlantic-cable.com/1858NY/index.htm (May 26, 2016).

Epilogue: The Finest Building in America

1. Kenan's ad appeared in the *New-York Daily Times* for Oct. 11, 1858. To the best of my knowldge, his photos have not survived.

2. *Scientific American,* Mar. 19, Apr. 9, Jun. 4, 1853; *The American Phrenological Journal* (Nov. 1858); Goodrich, *Science and Mechanism*,

106. Cf. the letter from "A Looker-On," probably Carstensen, which complains of *New-York Daily Times,* Jul. 20, 1853. Sedgwick admitted that there had been problems because they had ordered iron "from different places, and it was found not to fit." "Lord Acton's American Diaries," 730. The Introduction to B. Silliman Jr. and C. R. Goodrich (eds.), *The Illustrated Record*, 33, attributes unspecified "prominent difficulties" in erecting the Crystal Palace to the fact that few Americans at the time understood iron construction. Also noteworthy is the letter writer who reported that the Crystal Palace was "the hottest place in town" despite the use of translucent glass and the addition of ventilators. Condensation formed on the windows at night, "and water runs down in copious streams." The situation allegedly got so bad that fires were often built inside to dry out the place! *The Constitution* (Middletown, CT), Jul. 4, 1853.

3. *New-York Herald*, Oct. 24, 1858.

WORKS CITED

A. Manuscripts

Trinity Church Archives
      Diary of Morgan Dix
Museum of the City of New York
New-York Historical Society
      Crystal Palace Papers

B. Contemporary Newspapers & Periodicals

Alta California
American Phrenological Journal
American Whig Review
Barre Patriot
Boston Daily Atlas
Brooklyn Daily Eagle
Chicago Press and Tribune
Columbus Enquirer
Constitution
Farmer's Cabinet
German Reformed Messenger
Grand River Times

Harper's New Monthly Magazine
Hartford Daily Courant
Illustrated Magazine of Art
Illustrated News (London)
Illustrated News (New York)
Liverpool Mercury
Living Age
Memphis Daily Appeal
New-York Daily Tribune
New-York Daily Times
New-York Herald
Ohio State Journal

Putnam's Monthly

Richmond Inquirer

San Antonio Ledger

Scientific American

Southern Literary Messenger

Spirit of the Times

Sunday Albany Atlas

United States Review

Weekly Eagle

Weekly Wisconsin Patriot

C. Books, Theses, & Articles

Transactions of the American Institute of the City of New-York (Albany, 1855)

Statement made by the Association for the Exhibition of the Industry of All Nations in Regards to the Organization and Progress of the Enterprise (New York, [1853])

Description of the Mammoth Tree from California, now Erected at the Crystal Palace, Sydenham (London, [1857])

First Impressions of the New World on Two Travellers from the Old (London, 1859)

The Ladies of the Mission. *The Old Brewery, and the New Mission House at the Five Points* (New York, 1854)

Abbott, John Loraine. *The Wonders of the World* (Hartford, 1856)

Adams, Bluford. *E Pluribus Barnum: The Great Showman and the Making of U.S. Popular Culture* (Minneapolis, 1997)

Auerbach, Jeffrey "The Great Exhibition and Historical Memory," in Jeffrey Auerbach and P. H. Hoffenberg (eds.) *Britain, the Empire, and the World at the Great Exhibition of 1851* (Aldershot, UK, 2008), 89–112

Barnum, P. T. *The Life of P.T. Barnum, Written By Himself* (London. 1855), 386

Barth, Gunther. "Demopiety: Speculations on Urban Beauty, Western Scenery, and the Discovery of the American Cityscape," *Pacific Historical Review* 52 (1983), 249–66

Bellows, H. W. *The Moral Significance of the Crystal Palace* (New York, 1853)

Bender, Thomas. *Toward an Urban Vision: Ideas and Institutions in Nineteenth Century America* (Baltimore, 1975)

Berman, Marshall. *All That Is Solid Melts Into Air: The Experience of Modernity* (New York, 1982)

Bernard, Andreas. *Lifted: A Cultural History of the Elevator* (New York, 2014)

Blumin, Stuart M. "Explaining the New Metropolis: Perception, Depiction, and Analysis in Mid-Nineteenth-Century New York City," *Journal of Urban History* 11 (Nov. 1984), 9–18

_____. "George G. Foster and the Emerging Metropolis," in Blumin (ed.). *New York by Gas-Light and Other Urban Sketches by George G. Foster* (Berkeley, 1990), 1–61

[Bobo, William], *Glimpses of New-York City* (Charleston, SC, 1852)

Briggs, Asa. *Iron Bridge to Crystal Palace: Impact and Images of the Industrial Revolution* (London, 1979)

Buckley, Peter G. "To the Opera House: Culture and Society in New York City, 1820–1860," unpub. Ph.D. dissertation, Stony Brook Univ., 1984

Burrows, Edwin G. and Mike Wallace. *Gotham: A History of New York City to 1898* (New York, 1998)

Carstensen, Georg and Chas. Gildemeister. *New York Crystal Palace: Illustrated Description* (New York, 1854)

Chapin, E. H. *The American Idea, and What Grows Out of It: An Oration, Delivered in the New-York Crystal Palace, July 4, 1854* (Boston, 1854)

Cocks, Catherine. *Doing the Town: The Rise of Urban Tourism in the United States, 1859–1915* (Berkeley, 2001)

Coleman, Earle E. "The Exhibition in the Palace: A Bibliographical Essay," *Bulletin of the New York Public Library*, 64 (September 1960), 459–77

Cutler, Edward S. *Recovering the New: Transatlantic Roots of Modernism* (Lebanon, NH, 2003)

_____. "Passage to Modernity: Leaves of Grass and the 1853 Crystal Palace Exhibition in New York." *Walt Whitman Quarterly Review* 16 (Fall 1998), 65–89

Dalzell, Robert F. *American Participation in the Great Exhibition of* 1851 (Amherst, MA, 1960)

Dulles, Foster Rhea. *Americans Abroad: Two Centuries of European Travel* (Ann Arbor, 1964)

Dupont, Brandon, et al., "The Long Term Rise in Overseas Travel by Americans, 1820–2000," *Economic History Review* 65 (Feb. 2012), 144–67

Ernst, Dorothy J. "Daniel Wells, Jr.: Wisconsin Commissioner to the Crystal Palace Exhibition of 1851," *Wisconsin Magazine of History* 42 (Summer, 1959)

Evans, Meryle R. "Knickerbocker Hotels and Restaurants, 1800–1850," *New-York Historical Society Quarterly* 36 (Oct. 1952), 376–409

Ffrench, Yvonne. *The Great Exhibition: 1851* (London, 1951)

Foner, Philip S. *Business and Slavery: The New York merchants & the irrepressible conflict* (Chapel Hill, 1941)

Foster, George. *Fifteen Minutes around New York* (New York, 1856)

Franklin, John Hope. *A Southern Odyssey* (Baton Rouge, 1976)

Gassan, Richard. *The Birth of American Tourism: New York, the Hudson Valley, and American Culture, 1790–1830* (Amherst, MA, 2008)

_____. "The First American Tourist Guidebooks," *Book History* 8 (2005), 51–7

Gayle, Carol and Margot Gayle. "The Emergence of Cast-Iron Architecture in the United States: Defining the Role of James Bogardus," APT Bulletin 29, no. 2 (1998), 5–12

Genin, John. *Illustrated History of the Hat* (New York, 1848)

Gibbs-Smith, C. H. *The Great Exhibition of 1851* (London, 1950)

Gilje, Paul. *Rioting in America* (Bloomington, 1996)

Gray, Lee E. *From Ascending Rooms to Express Elevators: A History of Passenger Elevator in the 19th Century* (Mobile, 2002)

Greeley, Horace. *Recollections of a Busy Life* (New York, 1869)

_____. *Glances at Europe*, 3rd ed. (New York, 1852)

_____. *Art and Industry As Represented in the Exhibition at the Crystal Palace, New York—1853–4* (New York, 1853)

Green, Vivien. "Hiram Powers's *Greek Slave*: Emblem of Freedom," *The American Art Journal* 14 (Autumn 1982), 31–39

[Hall, Eldon], *A Condensed History of the Origination, Rise, Progress and Completion of the "Great Exhibition of the Industry of All Nations," Held in the Crystal Palace, London* (Redfield, NY, 1852)

Harrris, Neil. *Humbug: The Art of P.T. Barnum* (Chicago, 1973), 147–4

Hirschfeld, Charles. "America on Exhibition: The New York Crystal Palace," *American Quarterly,* 9 (Summer, 1959), 101–16.

Hobhouse, Christopher. *1851 and the Crystal Palace* (New York, 1937)

Hobsbawm, Eric. *The Age of Capital, 1848–1875* (New York, 1975)

Hofstadter, Richard and Michael Wallace (eds.), *American Violence: a Documentary History* (New York, 1970)

Huston, James L. *The Panic of 1857 and the Coming of the Civil War* (Baton Rouge, 1987)

Hyman, Linda. *Crystal Palace/42nd St./1853–54* (New York, 1974)

_____. "The *Greek Slave* by Hiram Powers: High Art as Popular Culture," *Art Journal* 35 (Spring 1976), 216–23

Jaffe, David (cur.), Bard Graduate Center exhibition *Visualizing 19th-Century New York,* 2014. http://visualizingnyc.org/about

James, Henry. *A Small Boy and Others* (New York, 1913)

Jayne, Thomas Gordon. "The New York Crystal Palace: An International Exhibition of Goods and Ideas," unpublished M.A. thesis, University of Delaware, 1990

Kasson, Joy S. *Marble Queens and Captives: Women in Nineteenth-Century American Sculpture* (New Haven, 1990)

Katz, Michael R. "But This Building—What on Earth Is It?" *New England Review* 23 (Winter 2002), 65–77

_____. "The Russian Response to Modernity: Crystal Palace, Eiffel Tower, Brooklyn Bridge," *Southwest Review* 93 (2008), 44–57

Kihlstedt, Folke T. "The Crystal Palace," *Scientific American* 251 (Oct 1, 1984), 132–43

Kilfeather, Siobhán. *Dublin: A Cultural History* (New York, 2005)

Kramer, Ellen W. "Contemporary Descriptions of New York City and Its Public Architecture ca. 1850," *Journal of the Society of Architectural Historians* 27 (Dec. 1968), 264–80

Leapman, Michael. *The World for a Shilling: How the Great Exhibition of 1851 Shaped a Nation* (London, 2001)

Le Duc, William G. "Minnesota at the Crystal Palace Exhibition, New York, 1853," *Minnesota History Bulletin* 1 (Aug.1916), 351–68.

LeMaster, J. R. and James D. Wilson (eds.), *The Mark Twain Encyclopedia* (New York, 1993)

Lockwood, Allison. *Passionate Pilgrims: The American Traveler in Great Britain, 1800–1914* (Cranbury, NJ, 1981)

Luckhurst, Kenneth. *The Story of Exhibitions* (London, 1951)

McNamara, Brooks. *Day of Jubilee: The Great Age of Public Celebrations in New York, 1788–1909* (New Brunswick, 1997)

Mulvey, Christopher. *Anglo-American Landscapes: A Study of 19th Century Anglo-American Travel Literature* (New York, 1963)

Nasar, Sylvia. *Grand Pursuit: The Story of Economic Genius* (New York, 2011)

Nevins, Allan and Milton Halsey Thomas (eds.) *The Diary of George Templeton Strong*, 4 vols. (New York, 1952)

Nichols, Roy F. *Franklin Pierce, Young Hickory of the Granite Hills* (Philadelphia, 1958)

O'Connell, Shaun. *Remarkable, Unspeakable New York: A Literary History* (Boston, 1995).

Penner, Barbara. *Newlyweds on Tour: Honeymooning in Nineteenth-Century America* (Durham, NH, 2009)

Pessen, Edward. *Riches, Class, and Power Before the Civil War* (New York, 1972)

Phelps, Humphrey. *The Lions of New York: Being a Guide to Objects of Interest in and around the Great Metropolis* (New York, 1853)

Pinchot, Gifford. *A Short Account of the Big Trees of California* (Washington, D.C., 1900)

Plunz, Richard. "City: Culture: Nature: The New York Wilderness and the Urban Sublime," in Madsen, Peter and Richard Plunz (eds.), *The Urban Lifeworld: Formation, Perception, Representation* (London, 2002)

Reps, John W. *Views and Viewmakers of Urban America* (Columbia, MO, 1984)

_____. *Bird's Eye Views: Historic Lithographs of North American Cities* (New York, 1998).

Reynolds, John. *Sketches of the Country on the Northern Route from Belleville, Illinois, to the City of New York, and Back by the Ohio Valley, Together with a Glance at the Crystal Palace* (Belleville, IL, 1854)

Richards, William C. (ed.) *Official Catalogue of the New-York Exhibition of the Industry of All Nations* (New-York, 1853)

_____. *A Day in the New York Crystal Palace, and How to Make the Most of It* (New York, 1853)

Robertson, James. *A Few Months in America* (London, 1855)

Jeff L. Rosenheim, "'A Palace for the Sun': Early Photography in New York City," in Catherine H. Voorsanger and John K. Howat (eds.), *Art and the Empire City: New York, 1825–1861* (New York, 2000), 226–41

Russell, Daniel E. "Crystals at the Crystal Palace: The Mineralogical Display at the 1853 Crystal Palace Exhibit in New York City," mindat. org/article.php/196/

Rydell, Robert W. and Nancy Gwinn (eds.), *Fair Representations: World's Fairs and the Modern World* (Amsterdam, 1994)

_____. *The Book of Fairs: Materials about World's Fairs, 1834–1916, in the Smithsonian Institution Libraries,* with an introductory essay by Robert W. Rydell (Chicago, 1992)

Scobey, David M. *Empire City: The Making and Meaning of the New York City Landscape* (Philadelphia, 2002)

_____. "Nymphs and Satyrs: Sex and the Bourgeois Public Sphere in Victorian New York," *Winterthur Portfolio* 3 (Spring 2002), 43–66

Sears, John F. *Sacred Places: American Tourist Attractions in the Nineteenth Century* (New York, 1989)

Silliman, B. and C.R. Goodrich (eds.), *The World of Science, Art, and Industry, Illustrated from Examples in the New-York Exhibition, 1853–54* (New York, 1854); originally issued in parts as *The Illustrated Record of the New York Exhibition of the Industry of All Nations*

Smith, John Jay. *Recollections of John Jay Smith* (Philadelphia, 1892)

Spann, Edward K. *The New Metropolis: New York City, 1840–1857* (New York, 1981)

Sperber, Jonathan. *Karl Marx: A Nineteenth-Century Life* (New York, 2013)

Steen, Ivan D. "Palaces for Travelers: New York City Hotels in the 1850's As Viewed by British Visitors," *New York History* 51 (Apr. 1970), 269–86

Swett, Richard N. "Georg Carstensen and the New York Crystal Palace," in Richard N. Swett and Colleen M Thornton, *Leadership by Design: Creating an Architecture of Trust* (Atlanta, 2005), 25–30

[Tappan, Lewis], *The Fugitive Slave Bill: Its History and Unconstitutionality, with An Account of the Seizure and Enslavement of James Hamlet* (New York, 1850)

George R. Taylor, "Gaslight Foster: A New York 'Journeyman Journalist' at Mid Century," *New York History* 58 (Jul. 1977), 297–312

Tolles, Thayer. "Modeling a Reputation: The American Sculptor and New York City," in Catherine H. Voorsanger and John K. Howat (eds.), *Art and the Empire City: New York, 1825–1861* (New York, 2000), 135–167

Voorsanger, Catherine H. "'Gorgeous Articles of Furniture': Cabinetmaking in the Empire City," in Voorsanger and John K. Howat (eds.), *Art and the Empire City: New York, 1825–1861* (New York, 2000), 287–325

Watson, John F. *Historic Tales of Olden Time: Concerning the Early Settlement and Advancement of New-York City and State* (New-York, 1832)

Weddle, Kevin J. *Lincoln's Tragic Admiral: The Life of Samuel Francis Du Pont* (Charlottesville, 2005)

Weightman, Gavin. *The Industrial Revolutionaries: The Making of the Modern World, 1776–1914* (New York, 2007)

Weisman, Winston. "Commercial Palaces of New York: 1845–1875," *The Art Bulletin* 36 (Dec. 1954), 285–302

Wilentz, Sean. *Chants Democratic: New York City and the Rise of the American Working Class, 1788–1850* (New York, 1984)

Martin Zerlang, "Urban Life as Entertainment: New York and Copenhagen in the Mid-nineteenth Century," in Peter Madsen and Richard Plunz (eds.), *The Urban Lifeworld: Formation, Perception, Representation* (London, 2002), 314–29

INDEX

Note: Page numbers in *italics* indicate photographs, illustrations, and captions.